On the Threshold of Grace

Methodist Fundamentals

Donald W. Haynes

"When first sent forth to minister the word,
Say, did we preach ourselves, or Christ the Lord?
Was it our aim disciples to collect
To raise a party, or to found a sect?
No, but to spread the power of Jesus' name,
Repair the walls of our Jerusalem
Revive the piety of ancient days,
And fill the earth with our Redeemer's praise."

— Charles Wesley, 1743

Printed in the United States of America

Published by UMR Communications

1221 Profit Drive

Dallas, TX 75247 U.S.A.

ISBN: 978-0-9845499-1-7

ENDORSEMENTS FOR THIS BOOK

"Don Haynes writes out of deep commitment to Jesus the Christ and to the Church in which he has served for his entire life, the United Methodist Church. This collection of essays provides a helpful view into the core beliefs and practices, and the uniqueness of this Wesleyan approach to living the way of Jesus. From a lifetime of experience as pastor and teacher, Don shapes these insightful and hopeful chapters at precisely the time we United Methodists seek to clarify our thinking."

Bishop Larry M. Goodpaster
Western North Carolina Conference, President, Council of Bishops
The United Methodist Church

"Any reader will profit spiritually from reading Donald Haynes' book, On The Threshold of Grace. The author grapples seriously with the contemporary meaning and application of historic Wesleyan concepts that have always been central to the tradition and without which one is hard pressed to claim 'a Methodist' heritage. The fast-moving text is filled with lively personal interpretations and illustrations that will draw the reader into a similar grappling with the Wesleyan view of the biblical gospel, which certainly will enliven and enrich their own Christian experience."

Richard P. Heitzenrater
William Kellon Quick professor of church history and Wesley studies
The Divinity School, Duke University

"an engaging, lively and faithful reaffirmation and fresh rendering of the marks, essentials, and distinguishing beliefs of the people(s) called Methodist. An exercise in self-definition that goes back to John Wesley and has been updated time and time again by successive spokespersons. Laity will treasure, and those on ordination track will appreciate, this readable essay on our evangelistic doctrines."

Russell R. Richey
William R. Cannon Distinguished Professor of Church History
Candler School of Theology, Emory University

"This book will nourish your mind, nurture your soul, and inspire your heart. Read it to learn, and study it to enjoy both success and significance in life."

Nido Qubein
President, High Point University

In Memoriam

Treva Joy Williams Haynes
1897-1989

Winnie Mae Lawing Parker
1906-1998

Joan's and my mothers who rocked us

In Methodist cradles

Nurtured us in John Wesley

And led us to Christ

TABLE OF CONTENTS

INTRODUCTION

"By rule they eat, by rule they drink,
Do all things else by rule, they think—
Method alone must guide 'em all,
Whence Methodists themselves they call."[1]

Millions today feel that life has lost its meaning, its purpose, its core beliefs. In a culture with more stress yet less meaning, people yearn for the anchor of certainties. **When we are adrift at sea, we will grab any piece of flotsam for a lifesaver.** Any preacher, author, or denomination that provides this guarantee of religious absolutism will undoubtedly make converts in a world awash with relativism. In the current religious marketplace, we cannot afford to ignore the erosion of Methodist influence among those who see...ore meaningful faith. Rather, Methodism must renew its "experimental divinity," match it with visionary confidence, and revive its mission — to follow Jesus, make disciples, and transform the world.

The message of Methodism has been blurred. We have retained our earlier methodology, but let our message erode. William Abraham, a son of Irish Methodism who now teaches at Perkins, laments Methodism's "doctrinal amnesia." Russell Richey, a pre-eminent historian of American United Methodism, said in a 2009 Wesley Study Seminar, "The emphasis of Methodism in the 19th century was missions and evangelism, **and in the 20th century was ecumenism."** I believe the hour has come, in the words of Isaac, to "redig the wells of our fathers" and re-state Methodism's fundamentals. While Methodism gives those who differ with us the freedom to have their own opinions, it does not mean that we have none of our own!

The intent of this book is to guide the individual reader or the small group in a recovery of John Wesley's "scriptural way of salvation."

We use the term "Methodist" generically rather than to identify a specific denomination. Wesley's grace theology formed and still influences the doctrine of all denominations whose doctrinal heritage is Arminian rather than Calvinist. In this volume, we limit "Methodist fundamentals" to doctrine as it relates to our personal faith journey. Some use the term "God's plan of salvation." We see "plan" as a corporate term and "way" as a relational term; so Wesley spoke of "*via salutis*" or "way of salvation."

Faith for Wesley was grounded in God's indefatigable love. This is the Wesleyan way to a purpose-driven life." But one need not be a methodist to find the Wesleyan journey helpful. We acknowledge that God's light shines from many lamps. We therefore hope the book will be helpful to those who look to other mentors for the God's Word that is a "lamp for our feet and a light for our pathway." If you are searching the Scriptures for your own salvation or "on the journey" in search of a meaningful life, may God add God's blessing to these pages.

United Methodist Bishop Kenneth Carder has observed that of questions coming to his desk as bishop, "Eighty per cent focused on theology, beliefs and doctrines; very few questions were about structures, apportionments, or the pastoral appointment process."[2] Albert Outler must be given massive credit for calling Methodism to recover John Wesley's theology. Outler wrote, "Wesley offers a treasure to the church of tomorrow that will leave it poorer if ignored."

In the 21st century to date, most neo-evangelicals reflect Calvinism, not Arminianism, as they "write the script" for seekers of saving grace. The same is true with Fundamentalists, including bright young mentors on university campuses. The intent of these pages is to nudge Wesley into the discussion of what it means to see salvation as "grace upon grace."

Who is a Methodist?

In his old age, as Wesley was laying the cornerstone of Wesley Chapel in London, he asked rhetorically:

Q. What is Methodism? Is it not a new religion?

A. Nothing could be further from the truth. Methodism… is the old religion, the religion of the Bible, the religion of the primitive Church… none other than the love of God and of all mankind.[3]

In response to the rising tide of fundamentalism in the 1920s, Methodist Bishop Edwin Mouzon struck the proper balance between Methodist "fundamentals" and "Fundamentalism": "It is one thing to be charitable in reference to theological opinions, and it is another and a different thing to be lax."[4] He added:

Methodism lays down no theological requirement for Church membership and allows large liberty of thinking. But belief in the essential facts of Christianity is, of course, necessary to being a Christian. United Methodism rests on a solid foundation of Apostolic, Protestant, and Wesleyan fundamentals of belief, experience, and practice.[5]

Gilbert Rowe of Duke Divinity School gave us a timeless definition of Methodism:

It is the most persistent and successful attempt that has ever been made to separate between the essential and the nonessential, to concentrate upon the essence of the Christian religion… Having learned that salvation is the possession of the Spirit of Jesus through experience, Methodism intends to allow nothing to interfere with or obscure this truth. The culminating doctrine of Methodism is the witness of the Spirit.[6]

In *The Faith We Declare*, Edwin Lewis wrote in 1939, "'In Christ' is the relationship by whose light we read God, and in whose light we will read ourselves."[7] Seventy years later, this remains a methodist fundamental. The world is waiting for a church that can market that message!

Former Duke Divinity School Dean Robert Cushman quotes from and comments on Wesley's letter to Conyers Middleton:

> "To believe (in the Christian sense) is, then, to... have a clear sight of God, and confidence in the most High, reconciled to me through the Son of his Love." Accordingly, it is manifest to the Wesleys that saving faith is the effectual work of the Holy Spirit and... the believer has a sure confidence that his sins are forgiven and he is reconciled. Wesley had not known this himself until 1738, but he then found it to be 'the *fundamental doctrine*' of the Church, the 'scriptural way of salvation,' and, along with sanctification, the 'core doctrine of experimental and practical divinity.'[8]

"If there were no sin," Cushman added, "there would be no relevance of this gospel, but since sin is rampant in every generation, the Methodists believe that the truth of this gospel is best expressed as 'taking the cure.'"[9] We believe that "living faith" is superior to simply a faith that is believed. To his former devotion to Scripture, tradition and reason, Wesley experienced grace at Aldersgate. He called the Methodist expression of salvation "practical divinity."

Ted Campbell, Perkins School of Theology professor of church history, is only one of a new breed of scholars who are taking us back to John Wesley. He writes, "In describing his vision of a catholic spirit John Wesley distinguished between essential doctrines and *opinions* about theology or church practices."[10]

Wesley's "Scriptural Way of Salvation"

In his posthumously published book, *Experimental Divinity*, Robert Cushman documented that early Methodism was clear about its doctrine. He called this consensus of faith *"consensus fidelium."*[11] He wisely proclaims that this consensus "embodies the 'sufficient reason' for a church's being" and prophesies that "the dimming, or decline, or erosion of that consensus is a negative prognosis for the survival of that church, particularly in modern secular society." He questions whether in the absence of this *consensus fidelium*, any

"Christian community can attain or retain a manifest identity and self-understanding, or convey a recognizable or enduring message, or, indeed to survive at all."[12]

Essential in the Methodist message is the inseparability of doctrines and personal discipline. Saying "Jesus has forgiven me of my sins" is just the first step in the way of salvation, not the *fait accompli*. Being saved must be followed by growth in grace, which expresses itself in the ethics of Matthew 25 and the discipline of Ephesians 6. Wesley insisted on doing no harm, avoiding evil of every kind, doing good of every possible sort, and attending all the ordinances of the Church. Through Bishop Reuben Job and others, we are recovering this imperative to "walk the walk."

As Randy Maddox, professor of theology and Methodist studies at Duke Divinity School, reminds us, "Wesley insisted on a dynamic interrelationship between God's justifying grace and our co-operant response."[13] Wesley connected "saving doctrine" with "living faith" as co-operant dimensions of the "scriptural way of salvation."

For Wesley, all doctrine must be "saving doctrine" and all faith must be "living faith," both of which were dimensions of a renovated life. Cushman closes the last book he ever wrote with ominous words, "The spectacular decline of membership in The United Methodist Church during the past decade and more may suggest that very many are wearied beyond endurance with a church that manages mainly 'the form of godliness,' on the one hand and seems doctrinally shapeless on the other."[14] We must hear that message.

Unlike Calvin who systematically wrote his "dogmatics," John Wesley was a preacher whose theology developed as his personal faith journey matured. Wesley himself first followed Jesus through personal and social holiness as a disciplined life. We see this from his university years through Aldersgate (1725-38). A number of his 'standard sermons' come from that chapter of his life. He was a devout man of God, but one thing he lacked — the assurance of saving grace and, as some of us sang while still children, "the peace that passeth understanding down in his heart." Perhaps the Achilles Heel of Methodism in modernity was the loss of what Methodist hymnwriter Fanny Crosby called "blessed assurance." We have lived within the boundaries of conventional morality, worked in the church or preached from the pulpit, but still lacked the confidence of faith that enabled us to bring others to Jesus.

The bottom line is that until the new Christian, the seasoned church member, or Wesley himself has an "Aldersgate" experience of knowing God's love, we will not have what Charles Wesley called "love divine, all loves excelling, joy of heaven to earth come down".

The time has come for all Methodists to do our homework, to stand up and to speak out! We must lose our timidity, get our message straight and share it — politely, respectfully, but with conviction. We must practice a radical hospitality that includes personal follow-up of worship guests and interpersonal faith sharing. We must preach the Good News!

Jesus met each person where they were; he did not have a "cookie-cutter" message or approach. Our evangelism begins in relationship and must remain there. We do not have a prescription "nor a sinner's prayer" nor "four spiritual laws" because we see neither of these in Jesus own evangelism. However, in the context of a caring relationship, there is a core message to convey. In these pages, we brand Methodism in the marketplace of religious theologies. We define our doctrinal fundamentals without becoming Fundamentalists. We claim the meaning of life in the context of God's saving grace.

Wesley summarized his theology as "grace upon grace." He used the metaphor of "porch" for **prevenient (preparing)** grace culminating in repentance, "threshold" for saving grace, and "every room of the house" for **perfecting** grace. By this metaphor he meant that God seeks to perfect us in love in every dimension of our life. We cannot grow in grace without spiritual discipline in a faith community. To "stay on the road," Wesley outlined what he called "means of grace."

Defining those means will be our final chapter. This book will take the reader down this road of "grace upon grace."

Methodism does not "cabin, crib, and confine" the work of the Holy Spirit. What Wesley called "the catholic spirit" is important: "If thy heart is as mine, give me thy hand." Wesley insisted, as we still must, "Though we may not think alike, can we not love alike?" If we present this as evidence that Methodists can believe just anything, we err. This does not mean, however, that we are a theological sieve or that we must remain mute about our beliefs. Wesley scholar and theologian Albert Outler distilled this for us with his insistence that Methodism has "a marrow of doctrine" that is distinctively Wesleyan and Arminian.

Indeed, Wesley warned against being "driven to and fro and tossed about with every wind of doctrine." He was clear:
> You who call yourselves of 'catholic spirit' only because you are of a muddy understanding, because your mind is all in a mist, because you have no settled, consistent principles, be convinced that you have missed the way; you know not where you are. You think you are into the Spirit of Christ when in truth, you are nearer the spirit of Antichrist. Go first and learn the basic elements of the gospel of Christ; and then shall you learn to be of a truly catholic spirit.[15]

> Neither does religion consists in orthodoxy or right opinions; which are not in the heart but the understanding... and may be orthodox at every point; he may not only espouse right opinions, but zealously defend them; he may think justly concerning the Incarnation of our Lord, the ever-blessed Trinity, and every other doctrine contained in holy writ... and yet it is possible he may have no religion at all...and may all the while be as great a stranger as the devil himself to the religion of the heart.[16]

Summarizing that sermon, Wesley said "true religion" was that point at which:
> God hath spoken to thy heart, Be of good cheer, thy sins

are forgiven. Thou hast righteousness and peace and joy in the Holy Ghost.... . Then the love of God is shed abroad in thy heart. Thou lovest him because he first loved us. And because thou lovest God, thou lovest thy brother also. Indeed thou art changed into that glorious image wherein thou wast created.[17]

Though Wesley's words use the medium of Shakespearean English, their message expresses the essence of Methodism.

The bottom line: Methodism has a doctrine, but we believe that true religion is not limited either to rational conclusions of the head or the enthusiasm of the heart. We believe in a marriage of the cognitive and the emotive, the head and the heart. Randy Maddox insists, "the mature Wesley integrated sacramentalist and evangelical emphases."

Author Diane Butler Bass, a former United Methodist herself, wrote in *Christianity for the Rest of Us*, "Few United Methodists can provide a conversational synopsis of 'who' the UMC is!" We want in the following pages to provide such a conversational synopsis! Between churches centered in sacramentalism and churches centered in enthusiasm, Methodism is a "middle way."

Notes on Revised Edition

The earlier edition of this book went through two printings. As I taught it in a number of places, I found myself needing rather substantial revision. Most of this consists of moving text to develop a smoother transition from one train of thought to another. I have also added more quotes from Wesley's sermons or journals at the beginning of each chapter and "Questions for Discussion or Personal Reflection" at the end of each chapter.

Questions for Discussion or Personal Reflection

1. What was said that prompted you to respond, "Amen! This is what I have been looking for!"

2. What prompted you to think, "Hmm. Interesting and helpful... never thought of that before?"

3. What bothered you most in this introduction?

4. What quote did you highlight?

5. How does your journey differ from this synopsis of what Wesley's calls "grace upon grace" or his metaphor of the "porch, the threshold of grace, and the house of many rooms"?

6. Does this introduction give you some clarity as to what the "consensus of faith" is for Methodism?

"My remnant of days I spend to His praise
Who died the whole world to redeem;
Be they many or few,
My days are His due,
And they all are devoted to Him!"

Wesley at 84
June 28, 1788

"I am a brand, plucked from the burning."

CHAPTER 1:
Methodism Begins With John Wesley

"I felt my heart strangely warmed. I felt I did trust in Christ, Christ alone for salvation and an assurance was given me that he had taken away my sins, even mine, and saved me from the law of sin and death."

— John Wesley, May 24, 1738

The message and mission of Methodism began with a man, John Wesley (1703-1791). We cannot define Methodism's fundamentals without reference to Wesley and his own spiritual journey. The foundation of Methodist doctrine is the Twenty-Four Articles of Religion that Wesley abridged from the Anglican Church. For the most part he deleted the ones which reflected the prevailing Calvinism of the Anglican Thirty-nine Articles…Thus our doctrine is rooted in a "middle way" between the Catholic Church's teachings about spiritual discipline and the Protestant Reformation's insistence on "justification by faith" — with an Arminian accent!

John Wesley was spiritually nurtured and psychologically shaped in a devout, learned, and rather rigidly disciplined Anglican family. His mother was as learned and well read as his Oxford-educated father. Both were very stern — not much affection was expressed in the Wesley family!

In the early years of Wesley's spiritual journey, had "the faith of a servant." The first "rise" of Methodism was at Oxford University— an academic setting that has remained influential in each generation of Methodist development.[1] Uniquely among founders of denominations, Wesley called for uniting "those two so long kept separate, knowledge and vital piety."

With his baccalaureate degree from Christ College, John Wesley became a deacon and priest in the Church of England, an ordination he retained until his death. He joined his father in Lincolnshire where he began a curate at Wroote parish. Then he was made a "fellow" at Lincoln College, Oxford in 1729, walking over a hundred miles to assume his new duties.

The term "Methodist" came from the derisive catcalls of Oxford University students who mocked the "holy living" of a campus group who were sometimes called "Bible Moths," "the Enthusiasts," and the "Godly Club." This evolved into the derisive term "Holy Club," which John Wesley himself never used—he detested the word "club" for an inclusive campus group. But the name that stuck from doggerel was "Methodists." Halford Luccock, a congregationalist, wrote of the Oxford Methodists:

> Colleges tend to turn out machine-made goods—graduates who dress alike, think alike, talk alike, act alike, and all on a dead-level of mediocrity. But every so often, there come men and women who refuse to wear the clothes, physical or mental, that are the mode of the moment. They lead a lonely life, but, as on the Lincoln College quad, future students and tourists will point to the bust under the windowsill of an ordinary dorm room and say, 'That is where the Holy Club met.'[2]

The second "rise" of Methodism was Wesley's twenty-two months of missionary ministry in Georgia (Feb. 6, 1736-Christmas Eve, 1737). General Oglethorpe appointed Wesley chaplain of the ship that would take him to his new appointment—Christ Church in Savannah, Georgia. On board ship were fifty-nine German Moravians. Before they left English waters he had begun to learn German in order to enhance his chaplain duties. En route, he was deeply impressed by the quiet resolve of the Moravians during a storm at sea.

As parish priest in Georgia, he continued his insistence that Christianity is a disciplined life of personal holiness accompanied by acts of Christian mercy, which he called "social holiness."[3] Wesley would weave into Methodism this Anglo-Catholic spiritual journey, which he always called "holiness of heart and life." During this time he searched the Scriptures, baptized babies by trine immersion, asked for confession before Communion if you had been absent a while, fasted, and met with the Moravians.

Returning to London in the dead of winter in 1738, he felt himself a failure and sought the spiritual counsel of Moravian Peter Bohler. Wesley's cognitive belief in Jesus as his Savior and his spiritual discipline were in place, but doctrine and discipline alone were less than satisfying. Wesley needed the confidence that God loved him. His troubled soul sought inner peace, and his anguish was in his lack of that "blessed assurance" that his sins were forgiven. Wesley's religion to that point has been a burden, not a delight. Walking the forty-three miles from London to Oxford, Moravian Peter Bohler said to Wesley what might be appropriate for many post-moderns today, "My brother, my brother, that philosophy of yours must be purged away."

The third "rise" of Methodism was the events leading to and following May 24, 1738. On that day after a spring of depression and rejection, he went as he wrote, "very unwillingly" to a Moravian small group Bible study and prayer meeting on Aldersgate Street in London. After years of spiritual journeying, Wesley finally reported that at "about a quarter to nine, I felt my heart strangely warmed." On that night his journey morphed from the "faith of a servant" to the "faith of a son." The watchword of Methodism became that experience of God's grace wherein we "know" our sins forgiven. Aldersgate was followed by Wesley's outdoor preaching and the beginning of "the people called Methodists."

Lovett Weems echoes all accurate readers of Wesley: "There is no way to understand anything Wesley said without first understanding his passion for a theology of salvation. His preaching was a preaching of salvation. His teaching was a preaching about salvation.

His ethics were ethics that emerge from the experience of salvation. His understanding of stewardship evolved out of his theology of salvation"[4]

These pages do not cover the range of all Methodist doctrine. This is a handbook of Methodist fundamentals regarding God's way of salvation as experienced and explicated by John Wesley, graduate of Christ College, Oxford; Fellow of Lincoln College, Oxford; Anglican priest; founder of the "people called Methodist."

Methodism has often ventured from what Wesley called the "scriptural way of salvation." But whenever we have recovered our voice, enjoyed the quiet confidence of saving grace, and folded assurance into discipleship, Methodism has had a vital message, seen lives changed, and greatly influenced societal culture. Therefore, we must look anew at who we are, what we believe, and what God is calling us to be and do. If so, in the words of William Sangster of London—"Methodism can be born again."[5]

Questions for Reflection and Discussion

1. What "new thing" did you learn about John Wesley in this chapter?

2. What made you most proud to be a Methodist in reading this brief overview of Wesley's life and spiritual journey?

3. The two mocking terms that the Oxford "Holy Club" was called were "Enthusiasts" and "Methodists." Do you think we would have "lived out our name" differently if we were "The United Enthusiast Church"? How so?

4. Discuss the three settings and developments that Wesley called the "rises" of Methodism—Oxford, Georgia, Aldersgate.

5. Note and discuss the import of Wesley's changing the chronology of the "order of salvation" in his own journey and the chronology he spelled out for us. *(Clue: For him "holiness of life and heart" came before Aldersgate; he sees that as the post-conversion chapter of our "grace upon grace" journey.)*

6. What disappointed you most in this chapter? How would you change it?

"I abhor the doctrine of predestination, a doctrine upon the supposition of which, if one could possibly suppose it for a moment (call it election, reprobation, or whatever you please, for all comes to the same thing). No scripture can mean that God is not love, or that his mercy is not over all his works. That is, whatever, it prove beside, no Scripture can prove predestination."

*"...**the soul that chooseth life shall live, as the soul that chooseth death shall die.**" This decree yields the strongest encouragement to abound in all good works, and in all holiness, and it is a wellspring of joy, of happiness also, to our great and endless comfort. This is worthy of God. It is every way consistent with all the perfections of God's nature. It gives us the noblest view of his justice, mercy, and truth. To this agrees the whole scope of the Christian revelation.*

"For if a sick man knows that he must unavoidable die or unavoidably recover, ...it is not reasonable for him to take any physic [medicine] at all. He might justly say, 'If I am ordained to life, I shall live; if to death, I shall die. So I need not trouble myself about it.'"

Thus our blessed Lord: "If any man thirst, let him come to me and drink." (John 7:37).

*Thus his great Apostle, Paul: "God commandeth **all** men everywhere to repent" (Acts 17:30).*

*Thus St. Peter: "The Lord is...**not willing that any should perish** but that all should come to repentance" (2 Peter 3:9).*

*Thus St. John: "If **any** man sin, we have an advocate with the Father...and he is the propitiation for...the sins of the whole world" (I John 2:1-2).*

—Sermon: "Free Grace" April 26, 1739

CHAPTER 2: Fundamental #1
Methodists are Arminians: What is That?

"I urge that… prayers be made for everyone, even kings in high places.…
This is right and acceptable in the sight of God our Savior who desires
everyone to be saved and to come to the knowledge of the truth."

—I Timothy 2:1-4

Arminianism is the paradigm for Methodist grace theology.
According to Wesley scholar Richard Heitzenrater of Duke Divinity
School, Wesley decided to meet the Calvinist challenge head-on
in November 1777 by producing a monthly magazine himself.
Wesley's distribution of "The Arminian Magazine" popularized
the work of Jacob Arminius for over a century. Heitzenrater says
Wesley knew Arminianism would offend some, but "was confident
that ninety-nine in a hundred persons in England rejected absolute
predestination and would thus not take offence."[1]

Jacob Arminius (1560-1609) was a Dutch Calvinist who became a
dissenter to the Calvinist notion of predestination. Wesley adopted
the doctrine of Arminianism and wove it into the theological fabric
of Methodism. Most Calvinist Christians know something about
Calvinism as a doctrine, but to many of us Wesleyans, the word
"Arminian" has no real meaning!

Arminians believe that God is all-powerful in sovereignty, *but we
differ from the Calvinists in how God expresses God's sovereignty.* To the
Calvinist, God expresses God's sovereignty in his omnipotence, his
power. To the Calvinist, God's sovereignty is expressed by "elective
grace." That is, every human being is so totally depraved and
deserving of eternal damnation that no one can "hear the still small
voice." Furthermore, if justice is served, everyone goes to hell. The

elect are saved; the rest get what they deserve—damnation.

We believe God chooses to express total sovereignty with total love for every one of God's children. That was the controversy in Wesley's day; that is the controversy in the 21st century. The question boils down to this: "Is the nature of God inherently justice or inherently love?"

Acknowledging that the Calvinists have their own scriptural proof texts, Wesley adroitly admits that he does not know the full meaning of texts like "God hardened Pharaoh's heart." Then he adds:

> There are many Scriptures the true sense whereof neither you nor I shall know till death is swallowed up in victory. But this I know, better it were to say it had no sense at all than to say it had such a sense as this. It cannot mean, whatever is meant besides, that the God of truth is a liar. No Scripture can mean that God is not love, or that his mercy is not over all his works. This is the blasphemy for which (however much I love the people who assert it), I abhor the doctrine of predestination.[2]

Jerry Walls, professor of philosophy of religion at Asbury Seminary, describes our issue with Calvinism this way:

> It doesn't do justice to the character of God revealed in scripture. It does not accurately portray the Holy One who is 'compassionate and gracious, slow to anger, abiding in love' (Psalm 103:8), the God for whom love is not merely an option...but who is such that his eternal nature is to love.[3]

Randy Maddox adds to that,

> The character of God and God's mode of relating to human beings was always at stake in his debates with the Calvinists. He insisted that God was not a despot who arbitrarily chose some for life and others for death. God's relation to humanity was expressed in Jesus Christ... 'Whosoever will may come' was the repeated theme.[4]

The Methodist fundamental doctrine, then, is that God is inherently love. Wesley's sermon, "Free Grace," preached in 1739 at Bristol, was published to refute Calvinism.[5] It begins "How freely does God love the world! While we were yet sinners, Christ died for the ungodly… and how freely with him does he give us all things! The grace or love of God, whence cometh our salvation, is free in all and free for all."

Wesley then asks the tough question, "But is this grace free for all, as well as in all?" He then defines what he sees as the essence of Calvinism: "By virtue of an eternal, unchangeable, irresistible decree of God, one part of mankind are infallibly saved and the rest infallibly damned; it being impossible that any of the former should be damned or that any of the latter should be saved."[6]

He concludes, "If this be so, all preaching is in vain." He calls predestination "a flat contradiction, not only to the whole scope and tenor of Scripture, but also to those particular texts which expressly declare, 'God is love.'" He quotes Psalm 145:9: "The Lord is loving unto *every* man and his mercy is over *all* his works." He refers to God's revelation to Peter that "God shows no partiality" as Peter was called to preach to Cornelius. Arminius, and Susanna Wesley in a letter to John in his college years, insisted that we must distinguish between God's foreknowledge and God's predestination. For God to know what choice we will make does not pre-empt our freedom to choose.

Then Wesley rolls out a litany of scriptural references to Jesus' death for "all," for "every man," for the "whole world." He refers to Jesus' invitation, "Come to me all you who labor and are heavy laden, and I will give you rest." He says if that weren't true, all references to God's weeping would be "crocodile tears, weeping over the prey which were doomed for destruction."[7]

We are not like marionettes on the end of a string pulled from above the stage! We can accept God's love or reject God's love. The word for this is synergism, Randy Maddox at Duke Divinity School calls synergism "responsible grace." Wesley over and again quoted John the Elder, "We love because God first loved us." (I John 4:19) Our response must be "in sync" with God's love.

25

In William Paul Young's *The Shack*, we see a clear picture of Arminianism in the context of bad things happening and Mack's protestations of his little daughter's murder. In an expression of good Arminianism, God says to Mack:

> Don't ever assume that my using something for good means that I caused it or that I need it to accomplish my purposes. Just because I work incredible good out of unspeakable tragedies doesn't mean I orchestrate the tragedies. Grace does not depend on suffering to exist, but where there is suffering, you will find grace.[8]

Until the 20th century, every Methodist was pretty clear on what it mean to be an Arminian. This recognition that we have a role in working out our own salvation creates moral responsibility. This we need to recover. To re-brand Methodism with its historic message, we must renew our understanding of God's sovereign nature as love and being made in God's image as having what Wesley called "natural liberty."

Why is it important to revive an old theological debate between Arminians and Calvinists? *Christianity Today* magazine recently had an image of John Calvin on the front cover with the headline, "John Calvin: The Comeback Kid." The magazine is correct; Calvinism dominates the neo-evangelical movement today. *Time* magazine ranked Calvinism third in its list of the Top 10 forces changing the postmodern world. Rick Warren popularized Calvinist theology in his bestseller, *The Purpose Driven Life*:

> Your parents may not have planned you, but God did. Long before you were conceived by your parents, you were conceived in the mind of God. God custom made your body just the way he wanted it. Many children are unplanned by their parents, but they are not unplanned by God. Your parents had just the DNA that God wanted to make you. He planned the days of your life in advance, choosing he exact time of your birth and death.[9]

Although Warren's book is apparently this generation's classic on the meaning of life in God's grand design, we Arminians do not accept his theology, which is called "monergism." As the prefix "mono" clarifies, in "monergistic theology," **God is the sole agent in every human event.**

At the Council of Dort in Holland in 1618, Calvinism was summarized in an acronym that is still used — Total depravity, Unconditional election, Limited atonement, Irrestible grace, and Perseverance of the saints. Glenn Hinson, a moderate Baptist who was once on the faculty of Southern Baptist Seminary, writes, "Fundamentalism of a more sophisticated sort traces its roots to **Dort Calvinism.** Albert Mohler, Jr, president of Southern Baptist Seminary, has been called by *Time* magazine, "the reigning intellectual of the evangelical movement in the U.S." He is described as a "cerebral, churchy…five point Calvinist" referring to the five points of the "Dort Calvinist" T.U.L.I.P.

We Arminians disagree with each letter! **The "T" stands for "Total Depravity."** We agree that the heart of the human problem is the problem of the human heart. Theologian Albert Outler says that from the image of God in which we were created, "Something has gone fearfully awry in the human enterprise"… . Yet Outler humorously notes, "we believe in total depravity, but not in tee-total depravity!" That is, we Arminians believe that while we are all sinners estranged from God, we can still hear the whispers of God's spirit. In St. Paul's words, "God's Spirit touches our spirits and confirms who we really are. We know who he is and who we are—Father and children" (Romans 8:28, *The Message*). God's love is a "hound of heaven" seeking love. If we listen to our soul at the "God moments" of our lives, we can "hear" the "still small voice" of God calling us.

The "U" in the Calvinist acronym **"T.U.L.I.P"** affirms their belief in **"unconditional election"** –that we are elected to be saved or lost, that we have no role in our salvation. God arbitrarily elects some to be saved.

The corollary to this is the **"L"** which might shock you! It stands for **"limited atonement,"** meaning that Jesus died only for those whom God elected to be saved. We Arminians believe instead that Jesus' atonement was not limited. We insist that Jesus died for every person, with no regard for gender, personal features, or "tribe." God's mission is defined in John 3:16: "God so loved the world that God gave his only Son that *whosoever* believes in him will have eternal life." That crucially important word "whosoever" means no limits; and whatever I have done with my life, "whosoever surely means me." Charles Wesley wrote this doctrine into many hymns, one of which is "Come sinners to the gospel feast; let every soul be Jesus' guest. Ye need not one be left behind, for God hath bid all humankind."

The "I" in the Calvinist acronym stands for their belief that grace is "irresistible." This is monergism, with God as the only agent in salvation. Arminians, on the other hand, believe that grace is resistible. God chooses to express his sovereignty with love, not power. God's love, like parental love, limits God's power at one point — what John Wesley calls "human liberty." That is, we have the free will to resist God's grace. Grace is the divine initiative to all; faith is the human response of those who so choose.

Let us be careful to quote Paul correctly: "We are saved by grace (God's initiative) **through** faith (our response)." The clue to the parable of the Prodigal Son's salvation is, "He came to himself and said, I will rise and go to my father..." The father had been waiting by the gate for years, but respected his son's human liberty enough to allow the boy to "come to himself." The son did not save himself; he realized his father's love.

The "P" in the Calvinist acronym "T.U.L.I.P." means "perseverance of the saints." The common parlance for this has been "once saved, always saved." Calvinism is a static relationship in which we cannot backslide. Considering the record of human behavior, we beg to differ. We believe salvation is a dynamic relationship, not a "once upon a time" *fait accompli*. Arminians believe that human nature being what it is, we can and sometimes do let our relationship with God atrophy and go dormant. Being a Christian means "walking the walk" as a follower of Jesus with his being the "pioneer and perfecter of our faith." To prevent backsliding, we need to practice what Wesley calls "means of grace" (see chapter 9).

Questions for Reflection and/or Discussion

1. Was the word "Arminian" new to you? If not, where had you seen or heard about it before?

2. Do you agree with Susanna Wesley's distinction between God's "foreknowledge" and God's "predestination" of all events?

3. Were you acquainted with the acronym "T.U.L.I.P" which continues to be used by Calvinists to summarize their doctrine? Which "letter," if any "turns you off" to what you believe about God and the work of Christ and our ability to resist grace?

4. Do you believe it possible for a person to be truly saved and then to backslide? If so, you are not a Calvinist!

5. Was this chapter helpful in defining a "Methodist Fundamental"?

6. As the chapter unfolded did you find yourself in agreement or disagreement with Arminianism?

7. Which passages of scripture will you underline in your Bible?

Like Thomas Aquinas, Wesley "divided" the love of God into "delight" which we find in God and "gratitude" which is our response to realizing that God loves us. "The numerous expressions of God's love on our behalf lay the strongest claim to our gratitude. Every reasonable person is to love God because his power, his wisdom, yea, and his goodness are infinite. 'We love Him, says the Apostle John, 'because He first loved us.'"

—paraphrase from sermon "The Love of God"

"Because they are children of God...they continually look up to God as their reconciling and loving Father (to whom) they cry for daily bread...."

—from sermon "The Marks of the New Birth" 1748

CHAPTER 3: Fundamental #2
"Way of Salvation" Begins With God's Character—Love

"God is Love and those who abide in love abide in God"

–John 4:16

"Thy darling attribute I praise, which all alike may prove,

The glory of Thy boundless grace, Thy universal love."

— Charles Wesley

All other major religions begin with a good man—Abraham, Mohammed, the Buddha, Confucius, etc. In Christianity alone the salvation journey begins with a good God! The invulnerable evidence is that we are called to a relationship with God who in Jesus Christ showed Himself a God of redeeming love. The God who is revealed in Jesus inseparably unites the incarnation and the atonement. The God-sent mission of the Bethlehem baby whose birth the angel announced as "good news of great joy which shall be to all people" is the same as the Savior of all humankind who died on the Cross.

We see the essence of the cross in Isaac Watts' words: "Did ere such love and sorrow meet or thorns compose so rich a crown *(as we see)* sorrow and love flow mingled down?" To quote "God" from *The Shack* again, "The God who is…'I am' cannot act apart from love!"[1] This is the essence of scripture's most familiar passage: "For God so loved the world that God gave his son" with the gift of amazing grace that "whoever believes in him will not perish but will have everlasting life." (John 3:16)

Albert Outler said at the Fondren lectures at SMU: "Even overwhelmed by our human lot with all our sin and life's tragedies, Jesus revealed God's love and, on the cross, demonstrated God's love, giving us hope beyond any human horizon—hope in, through, and beyond tragedy. The Christian gospel is not that Jesus appeased God's wrath on the cross, but that he was and is the agent of the Father's redemptive compassion."[2]

Charles Wesley spoke for any of us when we feel "down on ourselves" in "in a funk": "Amazing love, how can it be that thou, my God, shouldst die for me?" Ted Campbell aptly notes, "Our emphasis on God's love does not contradict our belief in God's power, but Methodist devotion stresses divine love."[3]

Almost all Christians will agree that only in Jesus do we see the perfectly revealed portrait of God. Jesus said, "Whoever has seen me has seen the Father." (John 14:9b) Then we must ask, "what kind of God did he reveal?" God is "Holy Will", but God is more than that! God is also "Holy Love." Because Holy Love can never be dormant, but must be expressed. John's Gospel prologue begins in the translation of J. B. Phillips, "In the beginning, God expressed himself."

 It is here that we discover and define the core "fundamental" of our belief: **God is love**. Gilbert Rowe of Duke Divinity School wrote: "Methodism learned and proclaimed the great truth that God deals directly with every [person] and is ready to impart to each one the best of all news—namely, that our sins are forgiven and each of us is a child of God."[4]

Millions of tracts have been distributed with what fundamentalists call "God's Plan of Salvation." Almost invariably, the first "point" is "You are a winner," quoting Romans 3:23, "All have sinned and come short of the glory of God." But Wesleyans do not use the term "plan of salvation." We use the term "way of salvation." The word "way" implies "journey" or "walk" rather than some word out of corporate culture like "plan." Parents don't have a plan for their children; they have a relationship. God created us for relationship with Him.

In William Paul Young's best-selling novel *The Shack*, God says to the argumentative Mack:

> True love never forces. Let's say it takes forty-seven life situations and events before you actually hear me. When you don't hear me the first time, I am not frustrated. That first time will be a building block to construct a bridge of healing that one day you will walk across.[5]

"'Tis Love, 'Tis Love, Thy Name is LOVE"

The first word in "the way of salvation" is not about us at all; **the first word is the character of God—love.** In the year 1050, a German Rabbi, Meir Ben Isaac Nehorai, wrote in Aramaic, the language Jesus spoke:

> "Could we with ink the ocean fill
> > and were the skies of parchment made
> Were every stalk on earth a quill,
> > And every man a scribe by trade
> To write the love of God above
> > Would drain the ocean dry
> Nor could the scroll contain the whole
> > Though stretched from sky to sky.
> O love of God, how rich and pure! How measureless and strong!
> > It shall forevermore endure the saints and angels' song."[6]

In his *Explanatory Notes Upon the New Testament*, Wesley's comments on I John 4:8 are noteworthy. Here in the writings of John the Elder is the Bible's only formal definition of God: "God is love." The Notes read:

> This little sentence brought St. John more sweetness, even in the time he was writing it, than the whole world can bring. God is often styled holy, righteous, wise, but…as He is said to be love intimates that this is His darling, His reigning attribute, the attribute that sheds an amiable glory on all His own perfections.[7]

Wesley says about John 4:19 —"We love Him because He first loved us"— that "This is the sum of all religion, the genuine model of Christianity. None can say more. Why then should they say less, or less intelligibly?"

In Charles Wesley's epic poem/hymn, "O Come Thou Traveler Unknown," we find this Methodist fundamental expressed so poignantly:

> … who seek thee, who art thou?
> Tell me thy name and tell me now…
> wrestling I will not let thee go
> till thy name, thy nature know…
> Speak, or thou never hence shall move,
> *and tell me if thy name is love*
>
> 'Tis Love! 'tis Love! Thou diedst for me,
> I hear thy whisper in my heart,
> The morning breaks, the shadows flee,
> pure Universal Love Thou art;
> To me, to all, thy mercies move—
> thy nature and thy name is Love."[8]

In John Wesley's "Sermon on the Mount VI," he says of the opening line the Lord's Prayer, "If he is a Father, then he is good, then he is loving to his children." He describes God as "our Father who day by day sustains the life he has given; of whose continuing love we know and every moment receive life and breath and all things. So much more boldly let us come to him, and 'we shall find mercy and grace to help in time of need.'" (Hebrews 4:16) We pray because we love, and we "love him because he first loved us" (I John 4:11).[9]

Bishop Scott Jones cites Wesley's sermon, "The Way to the Kingdom": "The substance of all is this, 'Jesus Christ came into the world to save sinners,' or 'God so loved the world that he gave his only begotten Son, to the end we might not perish, but have everlasting life'" (John 3:16). Importantly, John continues, "Indeed, God did not send the Son into the world to condemn the world, but in order that the world might be saved through him."[10]

God's love is neither elective nor selective; it is for all. Wesley's central thrust refers to Jesus' words, "If any man thirst, let him come to me and drink" (John 7:37). He loves one of the latest written of all New Testament verses, "the Lord is not willing that any should perish, but that all should come to repentance" (II Peter 3:9). He closes the sermon with a song hymn from Charles, "Universal Redemption." One line is "Come freely come, whoever will, and living water take." Charles also expresses this in his invitational hymn: "Come sinners to the gospel feast, let every soul be Jesus' guest/ Ye need not one be left behind for God hath bid all humankind."[11]

"For Wesley, grace is the manifestation of God's love,"[12] Bishop Scott Jones wrote. Over and over again, Wesley insisted that John 3:16 is foundational, and he placed this verse in tandem with John 4:9-10: "God's love was revealed among us in this way: God sent his only Son into the world so that we might live through him. In this is love, not that we loved God, but that he loved us and sent his Son".... A few sentences further John the Elder reminds us, "We love because he first loved us" (I John 4:19).

Rick Warren sounds like an Arminian when he writes, "God wants us to run to him, not from him. In fact 365 times in the Bible, God says, *'Don't be afraid.'* That's one 'Fear not' for every day of the year!"[13]

Wesley insisted that the capstone of being created in the image of God is being endowed by God with human liberty. When love is so thoroughgoing that it sets the loved one free, its power is compromised. In our freedom we can reject God's love. So love is a risk; love is vulnerable. In any relationship, divine or human, when love is rejected the initiator of love must make a decision—to continue loving or to withdraw love.

Human love is often conditional—"I will love you if…" or "I will love you so long as … " God's love is steadfast, unconditional, and never-ending. James Montgomery has us sing this:
"I know not how the island palms lift fronded palms in air.
I only know I cannot drift beyond God's love and care."

The love of God is portrayed poignantly in Jesus' parable that German theologian Helmut Thielicke correctly insisted should be called "The Parable of the Waiting Father." When Rembrandt was an old man, he painted his famous "Return of the Prodigal Son," an amazing revelation of the parable's deeper meaning. The central figure is not the son who has returned home, nor the sulking elder brother in the shadow. Rather it is the father, still wealthy as the red robe depicts, but now old and blind. The left hand is the strong clasping hand of a male; the right hand is the caressing hand of a woman! These were the hands that in love never let the boy go.

Rembrandt's painting gives no resemblance of a courtroom where justice is to be administered, or a mediator's desk where a deal is to be struck. The picture portrays nothing of a paternal lecture about bad behavior, immoral relationships, or squandered inheritance—or a demand that the son be willing to "obey the rules of the house" if he is re-admitted. Rather there is an overwhelmingly warm and loving welcome. As one studies the picture, the Scripture seems to appear before one's eyes: "My son who was lost is found. Put shoes on his feet and rings on his fingers and a robe his shoulder. Kill the fatted calf." Henri Nouwen's book, *Return of the Prodigal Son*, tells how the author's study of this picture changed his ministry and his life.

The same chapter of Luke that records the parable of "The Waiting Father" tells us, "There will be more joy in heaven over one sinner who repents than over ninety-nine righteous persons who need no repentance" (Luke 15:7). Maddox helps us see that Wesley's language about salvation is more therapeutic than juridical. Calvinism makes redemption sound like a courtroom where some are punished and some are acquitted; Wesley makes redemption more like a clinic where all the sick are being treated for healing. This does not mean that sin is psychological; it means that sin is what Wesley calls a disease, a corruption.

Far too many of God's children have lost their way in life. For some, that lostness has led to behavior they cannot change, substances they cannot kick, relationships they cannot break, habits they cannot overcome, and guilt they cannot shake. For some, life has simply lost its meaning. When we have lost our way, we cannot get home alone. Even the best of psychological counseling cannot do what a manifestation of the love of God can do.

We Methodists insist that Jesus did not die to placate the anger of God but rather to show us how much God loves us. As William Paul Young writes in *The Shack*:

> …my purposes are not for my comfort, or yours. My purposes are always and only an expression of love. I purpose to work life out of death, to bring freedom out of brokenness and turn darkness into light. What you see as chaos, I see as fractal. All things must unfold, even though it puts all those I love in a world of horrible tragedies—even the one closest to me.[14]

The character, Mack, in *The Shack* responds, "You are talking about Jesus, aren't you? What did he accomplish by dying?" God answers regarding Jesus mission: "The substance of everything that love purposed from before the foundation of Creation… Reconciliation is a two-way street and I have done my part. It is not the nature of love to force a relationship but **it is the nature of love** to open the way."[15]

In his *Explanatory Notes Upon the New Testament*, John Wesley's commentary on I John 4:8 are important to our journey. It is here that John the Elder gives the Bible's only formal definition of God—"God is love." Wesley's footnote:

> This little sentence brought St. John more sweetness, even in the time he was writing it, than the whole world can bring. God is often styled holy, righteous, wise, but here He is said to be 'love,' intimating that this is His darling, reigning attribute, the attribute that sheds an amiable glory on all His other perfections."

A contemporary "Christian Rock" song ends with the essential message of the Christian Gospel: "I hear you whispering my name. You (God) say, 'My love for you will never change. My love for you will never change.'"

From these diverse sources, we find testimony to Wesley's position that God's major attribute is love!

Questions for Discussion and Reflection

1. Believing that God loves us "warts and all" is not easy! Was this chapter helpful in take a new step in your own faith journey?

2. Which quote from other sources was most helpful?

3. Where did you find yourself in disagreement with the author?

4. If we don't love ourselves at this point in our journey, it is hard to believe that the holy God loves us. Can you believe that? Everything else in becoming a Christian or remaining a Christian rests on the premise that our behavior does not identify us—we are a child of God regardless of behavior and that is our identity. **Sign your name on a card you keep in your wallet:**

＿＿＿＿＿＿＿＿＿＿＿＿＿＿＿＿＿,

(son, daughter) of the Most High God,

made in His Image, redeemable by his Love

For Wesley, salvation begins with God's gracious, seeking love. The first quote clearly makes God the initiator of saving grace through "preparing" or "pre-coming" grace. There is no hint here of satisfying the wrath of an angry God.

"If we take this in its utmost extent it will include all that is wrought in the soul by what is frequently termed 'natural conscience,' but more property, 'preventing grace'; all the 'drawing' of the Father, the desires after God, which, if we yield to them, increase more and more; all that 'light' wherewith the Son of God 'enlighteneth everyone that cometh into the world,' showing every man 'to do justly, to love mercy, and to walk humbly with his God.'"

—from Sermon "Scriptural Way of Salvation"

Notice the language in the following quote. It is more like a clinic than a court!

"You are in the hands of a wise Physician, who is lancing your sores in order to heal them. He has given you now the spirit of fear, but it is in order to reveal the spirit of love and of a sound mind. You have now received the spirit of bondage; is it not the forerunner of the spirit of adoption? He is not afar off! Look up! And expect him to cry in your heart, 'Abba (Father).' He is nigh that justifieth."

—a Wesley letter to a seeker

Here Wesley is quoting a Quaker mystic:

"'My son, give me thy heart' is the language of the great God to every rational creature. 'Give me thy heart for it was I who made it, it was I that gave it to thee! It was I that bestowed its vital motion, and that for no other end but to direct and incline it toward me; I am thy true good; in me alone canst thou find rest for thy soul; all the springs of thy happiness are in me. Therefore...give me thy heart. Tis I alone who can reward thy love.'"

—Wesley's quote of John Norris (1657-1711)

CHAPTER 4: Fundamental #3

Preparing Grace — God's Love is a Seeking Love

"There is joy in the presence of the angels of God
over one sinner who repents."

—Luke 15:10

God's love is a seeking, pro-active love. In Genesis 1:27, we see that God created us in God's own image, in perfectly harmonious relationship. Then, in the creation story of Genesis 3, we read of the "fall" and the subsequent estrangement, alienation, and brokenness of this Creator-creature relationship. Sin is real and deep and destructive, but God never gives up on us! Our sin does not define us; our creation as a son or daughter of the most High God defines us!

Wesley did not minimize the pervasiveness of original sin, but as Wesley Theological Seminary professor Lovett Weems writes: "Sin is not what God wants for us. God is not content for us to experience nothing but the seductive pull of original sin. So God, even in our sinfulness, comes to us in grace."[1] As we sing our faith, we say that God comes to us in a "love that will not let me go; I rest my weary soul in thee."[2] God seeks us before we seek God. In Charles Wesley's account of his own journey, he says, "I heard thee whisper in my heart." God's grace is manifest to us before we have a consciousness of God's love for us, or any desire to follow Jesus. We cannot save ourselves. Paul says, "We cannot pray 'Jesus is Lord' except through the power of the Holy Spirit" (I Corinthians 12:3).

This first evidence of grace is what Wesley called "prevenient grace." It is entirely the work of God, the grace that "comes before," or "preparing grace." The United Methodist Article VIII speaks of prevenient grace: "We have no power to do good works…without the grace of God by Christ's prevening us (preparing us). As Weems teaches us, God comes to us first. Before we ever take a step, God is there. Within every life, from the beginning, is this simple, basic, elemental, initiating presence of God."[3]

Prevenient grace is entirely the work of God. God initiates; we respond. Author Steve Harper points out, "Prevenient grace is to some a novel idea, but it is crucial in understanding Wesley's order of salvation." Wesley called it "the awakening of the soul." This is grace "whispering to our heart," awakening our deadened natural conscience, which Wesley believed "is more or less uneasy when we act contrary to the light of our own conscience."[4]

I had the privilege of sitting under the teaching of British Methodist Rupert Davies, an expert in the mind and soul of Wesley. I heard him say what later appeared in his book, *Methodism*: "The relentless teaching about sin is alleviated by the consideration that fallen man still has the law of God written on his heart and a conscience with which to discern it."[5] Davies then gave us three prevenient gifts of God to fallen humanity: the moral "inner light" of **conscience**, the capacity for **reason**, and the **freedom** to hear and receive the Word of God. All of these played a pivotal role in the development of Wesleyan theology, and all lead us to very different conclusions about God's grace than does Calvinism.

In prevenient grace, Wesley is insisting that the image of God in which we were created is not totally obliterated. Salvation begins with God's loving, seeking initiative, even while we are still "dead in sin." In his sermon "The Image of God," Wesley preached from Colossians 3:10, "Yet our merciful, though rejected, Creator would not forsake even the depraved work of his own hands, but provided for him, and offered to him a means of being renewed after the image of him that created him."[6]

The United Methodist *Book of Discipline* includes prevenient grace in its lists of "distinctive Wesleyan emphases": "This grace prompts our first wish to please God, our first glimmer of understanding concerning God's will, and our 'first transient conviction' of having sinned against God."[7] This seeking love or prevenient grace is clearly an activity of God, but we can resist, refuse, and stonewall it. We can, in the words of an older Methodist generation "quench the Spirit."

As is so movingly portrayed in Holman Hunt's painting of "Christ at the Door," God's seeking love is seen in Christ knocking at the door, but the latch is on the inside. "With him who opens the door, I will come in and dine" (Revelation 3:20). We are not saved by our faith, but by God's grace through a faith that grace kindles, through a quickened conscience that amazing grace awakens. God's love is relational, and relationship requires two! To God's prevenient, nudging, whispering grace we can say "yes," or "maybe later," or "no." Grace is resistible; here we differ again from the Calvinists.

Asbury Theological Seminary professors Jerry Walls and Joseph Dongell created a novel piece of fiction that provides a picture of the God-initiated dimension of prevenient grace, in contrast to Calvinism's concept of elective grace.[8] They picture a prisoner held by terrorists for a long time in a dank cell. She has succumbed to the "Stockholm syndrome" and identified with her captors to the point that she makes no attempt to escape. Only an invasion from outside will rescue her.

The Calvinist view of divine invasion is simple: God invades the camp, swoops up the prisoner, strips off her shackles and blindfold, and makes her free, even though she does not want freedom. The rescuer is irresistible; she is freed against her will. God has been the lone actor throughout.

The Arminian view of the same scenario believes that God steals into the prison and makes it to the bedside of the prisoner. God begins to ask, "Do you know who you are? Let me tell you. Do you know what has happened to you as your captors have made you feel at home in this dark, dank cell? Let me tell you." Truth begins to dawn.

43

The Savior holds up a mirror and shines a light in it and she sees her sunken eyes and matted hair and frail body. God says, "Do you see what they have done to you and have you forgotten who you really are? Can I show you a picture of who you really are and what a great restoration to freedom and abundant life is yours if you come with me?"

The Rescuer presses on. "I know a part of you suspects that I have come to harm you, but let me show you my hands. See this blood. I crawled through an awful tangle of barded wire to get to you. I want to carry you out of here right now. Trust me. Put your arm around my neck and surrender yourself to me as we get to freedom." She could say, "No," but she responds to this seeking, rescuing care, puts her arm around his neck, and welcomes being carried from captivity to freedom.

This little drama portrays so well that we have been captured by sin and developed a comfort zone in our imprisonment. God seeks us out, whispers in our soul, and awakens us to the reality of our circumstances. Like the prodigal son who "came to himself," we do not resist rescue from bondage.

In Disney's "Lion King," Mufasa, the king of the lions, is killed, and his son, Simba, is cheated out of his inheritance. After Simba is transported through the land of the evil hyenas to the culture of the warthogs, he is comfortable in his new identity. Finally, Rafiki rescues Simba and tells him that he is not a warthog. Rather he is the son of the great Lion King Mufasa! He takes the young lion up to a rock ledge overlooking the vast jungle — Simba's rightful kingdom. Then comes the punch line from Rafiki: "Simba, you are more than you have become." That is precisely what the Holy Spirit says to us in prevenient grace!

In Wesley's sermon "Witness of the Spirit I," he stressed the priority of the Spirit's prevenient and direct witness as the necessary precondition to forgiving grace or "blessed assurance of knowing one's sins forgiven." Again, the bottom line is that prevenient grace is divine initiative, witnessing to us that we need not remain in bondage to sin. Logically, the sermon is based on Romans 8:16 — "The Spirit itself beareth witness with our spirit that we are children of God." The implication is profoundly important. Regardless of our sin, our addictions, or the number of people we have hurt; God love us and is proactively "whispering to our heart" that we are more than we have become.

There is so much good in what Rick Warren writes in *The Purpose of Christmas*, an example being:

> You were created as an object of God's love. He made you in order to love you. Every time your heart beats and every time you take a breath, God is saying, 'I love you.' He loves you when you don't feel his love as much as when you do. He loves you regardless of your performance, your moods, your actions, or your thoughts. His love for you is unchanging.[9]

Unfortunately, Warren immediately follows this beautiful insight with a brief return to his doctrine of predestination!

Prevenient grace also makes humankind morally responsible. That is, we can accept or resist the "still, small voice," the urge to repent, the mystical moment when God seems so near. That response is what Randy Maddox of Duke Divinity School names "co-operant grace." That is, we make a decision, a decision rooted in our God-given human liberty or free will. Because we are free to make the choice of our preference, it is moral. Perkins' William Abraham puts it so accurately: "Prevenient grace is the initial help God gives to everyone to see how grim things are and to form the first intention to get help."

God's seeking love has three dimensions. First, God gave us what Wesley called a "natural conscience." Wesley says of conscience, "Its main business is to excuse or accuse, to approve or disapprove, to acquit or condemn." He interprets St. Paul's understanding of conscience as "a faculty or power, implanted by God in every soul that comes into the world or perceiving what is right and wrong in his own heart and life, in his tempers, thoughts, words, and deeds."

Wesley explains that heathens are to be judged on the conscience that is universally "written on their hearts," but "the Christian rule of right and wrong is the Word of God".... This is the lantern for a 'Christian's feet' and a light in all his paths.

Secondly, prevenient grace brings us under conviction for our sin (a state) and our sins (the total package of our thoughts, words, and deeds). Every person has a kairos moment, a "God moment" if you will, in which our past rolls by us like an old movie, our present state is a posture of "I'll do it my way," and we have some fear of what is going on with us. In the old days, this was called "coming under conviction." It meant a moment of soul truth. This is the work of the Holy Spirit. As Abraham says it, God has stepped into everyone's inner life to help us see what is wrong with us and to awaken us to a positive response.[10]

Thirdly, prevenient grace comforts us. When we are in our darkest hour and our faith is very weak—our hours of distress, fear, and grief— God is with us in ways we cannot understand. Someone has said, "When we reach the end of our rope, God has already tied a knot in it." When we are at our lowest ebb, we sense some higher power undergirding us and giving us the courage to "soldier on." We all have seen the poem, "Footprints in the Sand":

> During the most trying periods of my life, there have been only one set of footprints.... Why, when I need you most, have you not been there for me? The Lord replied, The times when you have seen only one set of footprints is when I was carrying you.

Methodist Ira Sankey, song leader for evangelist Dwight L. Moody in the late 19th century, became acquainted in Scotland with a local poem comparing God's seeking love with the highlands shepherds' determination to never lose a sheep. Poet Elizabeth Clephane related that loyalty to the parable of Jesus in Luke 15. One night Moody preached on that text and for the altar call turned to Sankey and said, "Sing something appropriate." Sankey sat down at the piano, hit an A-flat and began to sing from his soul the words of Clephane's

poem to a tune never before rehearsed nor even created. It was
a miraculous moment. Thousands have come to Christ with this
poignant, moving narrative of God's highly personal, never-ending,
seeking love:

> 'Lord, Thou hast here Thy ninety and nine,
>   are they not enough for Thee?'
> But the Shepherd answered 'This of Mine
>   has wandered away from Me.
> And although the road be rough and steep,
> I go to the desert to find my sheep'
> But through the mountains, thunder-riv'n,
>   and up from the rocky steep,
> There arose a glad cry to the gate of heav'n,
> 'Rejoice I have found my sheep!'
> And the angels echoed around the throne,
> 'Rejoice for the Lord brings back his own!'

Francis Thompson, a Roman Catholic in London's Victorian age, was
a destitute, opium addict for years. He was rescued by a Christian
who reached out to him. Thompson's poem "Hound of Heaven" is so
poignantly descriptive of God's love:

> I fled him down the nights and down the days,
> I fled him down the arches of the years
> I fled him down the labyrinthine ways
> Of my own mind . . . and in the mist of tears
> I hid from Him and under running laughter
> Up vista-ed slopes, I sped;
> And shot precipitated….
>
> But with unhurrying chase and unperturbed pace,
> Deliberate speed, majestic instancy
> They beat—and a Voice beat more instant than the feet.
> (And God responds:)
> "All things betray thee who betrayest Me
> How little worthy of any love thou art!
> Whom wilt thou find to love ignoble thee,
> Save Me, Save Only Me?....

Oh that thou might'est seek in My arms,
All, my child you fancy as lost!
Ah, fondest, blindest, weakest,
I am He whom thou seekest!
Rise, clasp my hand and come!"

Fanny Crosby, a devout Methodist who was blind from childhood, gave us over 8,000 hymns, but none is greater than, "Rescue the Perishing," written in 1869. Listen to the contemporary idiom!

"Tho they are slighting Him still He is waiting,
        waiting the penitent child to receive;
Plead with them earnestly, plead with them gently;
He will forgive if they only believe
Down in the human heart, crushed by the Tempter,
        feelings lie buried that grace can restore
Touched by a loving heart, wakened by kindness,
Chords that were broken can vibrate once more."

Wesley preached "grace is for all and in all." The Holy Spirit quickens our conscience, whispers to our heart, and awakens our soul. God's is a seeking love that never gives up but never violates our human liberty to resist love.

Questions for Reflection or Discussion

1. Is the term "prevenient grace'" new to you? Does it help to substitute "preparing" for Wesley's word "pre-venient"? *(This obsolete word means "pre-coming" or the grace that comes before our repentance and "draws" us toward God's love.)*

2. At some "God moment" in our life, have you felt convicted of your sinfulness? At some "God moment," have you felt "washed whiter than snow" from your sin? If not, why not now? Finish your homework with God; your reward is "peace that passes understanding."

3. Turn in your Bible to Revelation 3:20 and get a Holman Hunt picture off the internet of "Christ at the Door." Have you unlatched the door from the inside? This is your role in salvation.

4. Rent "The Lion King." *Put in your name where Simba's is. Are you more than you have become?* Are you ready to "let go and let God"?

5. Have you ever heard Ira Sankey's "Ninety and Nine" sung? Can your identify with this portrayal of Luke 15:3-7?

6. Did you find Francis Thompson's poem, "Hound of Heaven" comforting or disturbing? The bottom line is like Psalm 139:7-12.

7. Fanny Crosby said of derelicts on skid row, "Down in the human heart, crushed by the Tempter, feelings lie buried that grace can restore." Whose loving heart and whose kindness can I awaken some perishing child of God to God's preparing ("prevenient") grace? Yours? What if your church's mission were to "flesh out" the message of Fanny Crosby's hymn, "Rescue the Perishing"?

"He (God) made man in his own image, a spirit endued with understanding and liberty. Man, abusing that liberty, produced evil and brought sin and pain into the world. God permitted this in order to (give us) a fuller manifestation of his wisdom, justice, and mercy by bestowing on all who would receive it an infinitely greater happiness…"

— Wesley, 1782

In Albert Outler's words, Wesley's sermon, *Original Sin, "in the logic of his soteriology, a major doctrinal statement in which he sought to compound the Latin tradition of total depravity with the Eastern Orthodox view of sin as disease, and is a sufficient answer to all simple-minded references to Wesley as a Pelagian."*

—Outler, *The Works of John Wesley,* V 2, Abingdon 1985, 171

CHAPTER 5: Fundamental #4
Sin is real — The Evidence is Clear!

"All have sinned and fallen short of the glory of God."

—Romans 3:23

The universal sin of which Romans 3:23 speaks comes third on our journey to salvation! In the words of Wesley's commentary, we have "fallen short of God's image for us." The word "fall" implies that we once enjoyed a higher level of relationship and spirituality. Wesley uses the term "original righteousness" to reflect our being made in the image of God (Genesis 1:27) and therefore sees salvation as restoration or healing following the fall.

Jesus said, "Whoever has seen me, has seen the Father." (John 14:9) As God stepped onto the stage of human history in the birth of Jesus, we saw God's true character: "God so loved the world that God gave...that we might have eternal life" (John 3:16). Now we must ask, "Just what kind of mess did God come into?" This brings us to the doctrine of "original sin" or "birth sin." Though we disagree with those who say that our sinful state is "No. 1," we also disagree with those who do not see the seriousness of sin. In the 1930s, while liberal theology was still strong in among theological faculties, Edwin Lewis wrote, "Christian truth has a certain organic character. Change anywhere affects change everywhere. Is it that they want the old terms dropped because they have ceased to believe in what those terms represent?"[1]

First, let's be clear about the "signs of the times" in which Wesley developed his theology of grace. The universities were dominated by the philosophy known as "The Enlightenment." A host of brilliant men updated much of Greek philosophy that, in Outler's words, "was a cherished conviction that men, once freed from their superstitious errors, would recover their innate moral virtue, viz. the power to will the good and to do it."[2] Wesley says, "Accounts of this kind have particularly abounded in the present century.... . Here not a few persons of strong understanding and extensive learning have employed their utmost abilities to show what they termed 'the fair side of human nature.'[3] If their accounts of him be just, man is 'a little less than God.' So it is now quite unfashionable to talk otherwise, to say anything disparaging about human nature."

Wesley then asks, **"In the meantime, what must we do with our Bibles? For they will never agree with this."**[4] This informed opinion documents that Wesley saw the error in the philosophy of the Enlightenment — a philosophy that would later erode the doctrine of original sin in Methodist Sunday school literature and Methodist seminaries. Edwin Lewis of Drew University called Methodism back from the "Enlightenment safari" with his book, *A Christian Manifesto*, in 1934: "Christianity is a religion of *regeneration*. You will believe again in the necessity and possibility of human nature being changed. The **necessity** of the change is in the fact of sin, both as a status and a deed; the possibility of change is in the nature of the grace of God.... . Deny the doctrine of sin and you will deny much more than that."[5]

From the late 19th century the wide and deep influence of the social sciences of psychology, sociology, and economics made the doctrine of sin either archaic or harmful. We saw this influence in the public school curricula which reflected John Dewey's progressivism. While we owe considerable debt to the social sciences, we must again the question Wesley posed, "But what shall we do with our Bibles?"

Edwin Lewis was not alone. Shelton Smith, professor of History of Protestant Thought at Duke, wrote six months before Pearl Harbor in 1941 regarding John Dewey's insistence on the "infinite value of human personality," "From the standpoint of the Christian faith, there seems to be no ground on which to say that human personality is of 'infinite worth.' Man is a contingent creature; in the Christian faith man is a theonomous being, deriving his meaning and value from his relation to God. When human personality is elevated to 'infinite value,' humanity is deified—made as gods."[6] He warned, "Those religious educators who renounce a theo-centric interpretation of the human situation are quite right in discarding the term 'sin.' They look only to the empirical sciences for their terms. Therefore they decline to speak of sin in its tragic dimensions. For sin becomes really tragic only to those who interpret it from the divine perspective."[7]

Lewis spoke prophetically a word that is an integral part of this book: "The time has come when the church must assert again... its right to deliver its soul on the great issues of life without first obtaining permission from some other sources."[8] Methodist Sunday School editors ignored the warnings of Lewis and Smith to our peril. Only by the 1960's were we hearing the trumpet sound again the doctrine of original sin. It was Albert Outler from SMU who shouted, "Something has gone fearfully awry in the human enterprise."[9] The doctrine of sin is fundamental; it affects every dimension of our theology.

Wesley insists that the doctrine of original sin is what separates Christianity from all other religions. His text for the "Original Sin" sermon is Genesis 6:5, which ends, "and that every imagination of the thoughts of his heart was only evil continually." Wesley's comment on that verse is, "Allow this and you are so far a Christian; deny it, and you are but a heathen still."[10]

If we are not sinners, we need no salvation! But we are sinners; our predicament is that of Paul in Romans 7 — "Is there no one who can do anything for me? That is the real question" (Romans 7:24, *The Message*).

In his sermon "Original Sin," Wesley supported St. Paul's conclusion: "So long as men remain in their natural blindness of understanding, they are not sensible of their spiritual wants..." Wesley says we can "acknowledge (God's) being, but have no acquaintance of Him. We can know there is an emperor of China, yet we do not know him."[11]

Wesley means we can have a cognitive belief in God but no personal relationship.

Steve Harper can be our teacher here by eliciting certain salient fundamentals from the whole of Wesley's writings.[12]

> "If sin were a 'thing' we could escape it, but because it is an infection, the only option is healing. We cannot try enough, learn enough, worship enough, or do enough good works to heal ourselves. Outside help is the only possible solution. The problem of sin infects the very nature of what it means to be human. Any attempts to remove ourselves from it are only exercises in futility. The solution is transformation, not escape. Wesley can help us out of our futile efforts to treat sin as a 'thing.' He keeps using the term 'disease' and pointing out that the only solution is 'taking the cure.'"[13]

According to Wesley, what are the symptoms of sin?

Sin makes us dead toward God. It gives us a false sense of security and peace. Wesley said:

> The poor, unawakened sinner has no knowledge of himself. He knows not that he is a fallen spirit. Full of diseases that he is, he fancies himself in perfect health. Bound in misery and iron, he dreams he is happy and at liberty . . . contented in his fallen state, to live and die without knowing he is made in the image of God, ignorant both of his disease and the only remedy for it . . .[14]

Wesley in another sermon warns that this "soul death" condition produces evil fruits: independence, pride, vanity, covetousness, lust, anger, envy.[15]

Sin is self-captivity. Thinking ourselves free, we become captives of our own reason, desires, prejudice, cultural blindness, and raw lusts — "prey to our own weaknesses." We are like Frank Sinatra sang in 1964 of his story: "I did it my way." He bragged that he was the master of his fate and kneeled to no one! In this state, we recognize no need for a Redeemer; there is nothing to be forgiven of. When we reach this low spiritual ebb, sin enjoys a reign of terror and wreaks havoc in our lives and those whom we influence most.

Sin is helplessness in the effort to change. Wesley did not believe that the image of God in which we are created is destroyed, but he thought it rendered powerless. Sin has done that to us. Wesley said, "Though he strive with all his might, he cannot conquer; sin is mightier than he."[16] Let us call for a reality check; we cannot pull ourselves up by our own bootstraps — the metaphor itself is ridiculous if one is sinking in quicksand. Our "free will" at this point is impotent. God's grace is essential.

Sin is our judgment of others. Did not Jesus say, "With the judgment you make you will be judged, and the measure you give will be the measure you get." In *The Shack*, Mack is told that his judgment is to become the Judge! He is told:

> You have judged many throughout your life. You have judged actions and motivations of others as if you really knew! You have judged the color of skin, body language, and body odor. You have judged history and relationships. You have judged beauty and righteousness by your concepts. By all accounts, you are quite well practiced in the activity.[17]

The Achilles' heel of 19th-century liberalism was looking at human nature through rose-colored glasses. Overlooking the "bent to sinning," liberal theology blamed the environment on everything wrong in society, from personal sin to systemic evil. On the eve of World War II, Edwin Lewis wrote:

> Much that we once called sin we today call by some other name, but changing the name does not change the dire reality itself. Frustrations, inhibitions, maladjustments, nonsocial attitudes — all these new ways of describing the ancient enemy of human peace and happiness in no wise do away with the enemy. St. Paul defined the gospel as "the power of God unto salvation to everyone who believes." The great task of the Church is to connect God's children with that power. The gospel of Christ can actually save

human lives and restore them to God. It can enable the drunk to attain sobriety; the thief to be an honest citizen, bring home the prodigal son, rehabilitate broken homes, strengthen weak wills, destroy hate in one's spirit, and create peace in troubled breasts. This is not mere verbalism; it is a sober fact of something that has been taking place for centuries and is still happening today.[18]

United Methodist Bishop Scott Jones points out that Wesley clarifies both **voluntary** sins (willful transgressions of the law of God). In this arena of our choices, Wesley includes "**inward sins**": our tempers, thoughts, lusts, and hate. Secondly, Jones clarifies that Wesley recognizes the inevitability of **involuntary** sins ("sins of infirmity because they arise either out of our ignorance or our being caught unawares").

Jones then reminds us that sin goes beyond the individual and infects the cultural. The great contribution of the 20th century to the concept of sin was to broaden it to include society's warped values of racism, sexism, the acceptability of pornography, "dirty jokes," and materialism.[19]

This affects every aspect of our theology. Bishop Kenneth Carder explains:

Sin has deeper roots than personal choices. This disease of the soul — sin — infects all human beings. It invades every aspect of life. Its power exceeds human strength and cannot be defeated by will power. Demonic forces pervade institutions, individuals, cultures, and systems. We fall victim to their prey without realizing it. The insidious powers of sin and death assault humanity with weapons of deceit, treachery, coercion, manipulation, and violence. The results are the persistent distortion of the divine image in humanity ...[20]

Goaded by theologians like Reinhold Niebuhr, United Methodist seminary faculties in the 20th century typically moved sin to the level of societal prejudices, systemic evil, and "tribal" prejudice. Many efforts have been and are being made to remove these injustices.

Contrary to some media voices, "social justice" is biblical. We need to read anew the book of Amos and Jesus' reading from Isaiah in his local synagogue! (Luke 4:18-21)

Ted Campbell's little digest of Methodist doctrine sums up our distinctiveness of the Wesleyan "way of salvation":
> "The 'way of salvation' is one of Methodism spiritual treasures: ...(it) seeks comprehensive transformation by God's grace. ...we should not only be inspired...as it appeared in the eighteenth century. We should be asking how people experience divine grace today."[21]

Let us do a reality check! Sin is personal and cultural. An important dimension of being saved is understanding sin—its persistence, perniciousness, and pervasiveness.

Questions for Reflection and Discussion

1. Do you agree that we need to face up to sin within the context of God's never ending love for us? Think about this in the context of parents and children. When children make a mess of their lives, do we want them to work through that feeling their parents are "out to get them and send them to hell" or will go to the threshold of hell to bring them "home"?

2. If you want to delve into a little history, compare the philosophy of the Enlightenment in Wesley's day and the philosophy of secular humanism today. Before you respond, read again Edwin Lewis' concern about "changing the name of sin" to "frustrations, inhibitions, maladjustments, and non-social attitudes." (*This is a question for "extra credit"!!*)

3. Read Steve Harper's quote again — "If sin were 'a thing,' we could escape it but because it is an infection, the only option is healing.[11] Have you ever before seen this distinction between a "clinical" and a "juridical" way of defining sin. One makes God the "Great Physician." The other makes God the "Judge." Where is your comfort zone?

4. Whether or not you read William Young's book, *The Shack*, how does the quote in which Mack is told that he is experienced in judging grab you?

5. Did older generations seen sin too narrowly? What was the "morality code" prior to World War II? What societal sins were accepted without comment?

6. Does the present emphasis on "social justice" tend to overlook the continuing necessity for "personal holiness"?

7. Prior to Aldersgate, John Wesley tried to "save himself" by "holiness of heart and life"—an almost monastic lifestyle. At Aldersgate, he recognized that only a divine "energy" beyond him could assure him of being saved. Only as we understand this are we ready for God to save us.

"…if you confess with your lips that Jesus is Lord and **believe in our heart** that God raised him from the dead, you will be saved. For one believes with the heart and so is justified and one confesses with the mouth and so is saved. The scripture says, 'No one who believes in him will be put to shame.' For there is no distinction between Jew and Greek; the same Lord is Lord of all and is generous to all who call on him. For, **'Everyone who calls on the name of the Lord shall be saved.'**"

— Romans 10:9-13

"If we confess our sins, he who is faithful and just will forgive us our sins and cleanse us from all unrighteousness."

— I John 1:9

"By his great mercy he has given us a new birth into a living hope…. Although you have not seen him, you love him…you believe in him and rejoice with an indescribable and glorious joy, for you are receiving the outcome of your faith, the salavation of your souls."

— I Peter 1:3, 8-9

"By salvation I mean not barely, according to the vulgar notion, deliverance from hell, or going to heaven, but a present deliverance from sin, a restoration of the soul to its primitive health, its original purity, a recovery of the divine nature; the renewal of our souls after the image of God, in righteousness and true holiness, in justice, mercy, and truth."

— John Wesley

CHAPTER 6: Fundamental #5
Saving Grace — Co-operant and Resistible

"Since we are utterly incapable of living the glorious lives that God wills, God did it for us! Out of sheer grace he put us in right standing with himself. A pure gift. He got us out of the mess we're in and restored us to where he always wanted us to be. And he did it by means of Jesus Christ... Having faith in him sets us clear."

— Romans 3:21-26 (*The Message*)

The lack of knowing the over-arching story of the Bible and the Wesley "way of salvation" leaves many Methodists easy prey for Fundamentalists when they ask the point blank question, "Are you saved?" If you say that you are, their clincher question is, "When were you saved?" We rejoice that many people come to Christ as personal savior at an identifiable time and place. However, for many of us, our journey begins in the earliest memories of childhood. The first time we "gave our heart to Jesus," might have been through the nurture of a parent, a Sunday School teacher, or some spiritual "significant other." Our creed is simple at that stage: "Jesus loves me; this I know for the Bible tells me so."

However, there comes that "God moment" in every Christian sojourner when we affirm "Jesus is Lord." Aha! That is "being discipled." Jesus said, "Learn of me." In what Rob Bell calls the "Eucharistic paradox," Jesus demands on the one hand, "Take up your cross and follow me." Paradoxically, it is liberating as he says what no other master will say: "My yoke is easy and my burden is light. I am come that you might have a more abundant life." As a new or "old" Christian we appropriately sing, "Jesus, Savior, pilot me over life's tempestuous sea." In reality then, an honest answer that reflects New Testament and Christian biography would be "Yes,

I am saved, and I am being saved, and I will be saved."

In Wesley's sermon "Justification by Faith," he begins by re-telling what we now call the great "meta-narrative" on which the Christian faith is based. As Wesley did repeatedly, we post-moderns must rehearse the Christian meta-narrative ("big story"). Without understanding it, the gospel does not "compute."

The Faith Meta-Narrative According to Wesley

Wesley preached on the "general ground of this whole doctrine of justification." Here is my paraphrase of his summary:

In the image of God man was made. (Genesis 1:27) Therefore Adam experienced God as love. Adam (*representative of all humankind on the morning of creation*) lived in love, dwelling in harmony with God, Eve, and creation. He was accordingly pure as God is pure. Such then was the state of man in the Garden of Eden — holy, happy, knowing and loving…. To maintain this relationship, God only gave one prohibition — *to be "as God" by eating the fruit of the "Tree of the Knowledge of Good and Evil."* (Genesis 3) Man disobeyed that prohibition and ate of the tree of which God had forbidden. *Eve did and Adam did; we call this "The Fall."* Thus by one man sin entered the world and became resistant to God's presence in his heart, insisting, "I'll do it my way." We still live out this narrative in our own life story. We call it "original sin."

The Biblical meta-narrative continues. From Genesis 3 to the angel's appearance to Mary as recorded in Matthew, this was the story of humanity's alienation from God. God gave the Torah ("instruction" or law of Moses, including the Ten Commandments) and the prophets but disobedience continued. The "law and the prophets" made little dent in history. The Hebrews were what Moses called a "stiff-necked" people.

The Hebrew Bible is filled with warnings that disaster is coming. Most scholars believe that Daniel was the last of the Hebrew Bible books because it was written in Aramaic, the language Jesus spoke. Pagans owned the Temple; Antiochus Epiphanes placed his own statue where the Ark of the Covenant had been! Daniel prays, "We have not listened to your servants the prophets who spoke in your name to our kings, our princes, our ancestors and all the people of the land. Righteousness is on your side, O Lord, but open shame falls on us." (Daniel 9:6-7) The old world was weary.

"But when the fullness of time had come, God sent his Son…so that we might receive adoption as children." Galatians 4:4). Jesus came as a second "Adam," the a redemptive "common head" of humankind, a second general parent representative of the race. In Christ, God was reconciling his estranged, alienated children to himself. The consequent story is that "as by the offence of one sin came, by the righteousness of the second came the free gift of justification." (Romans 5:18b)

But even the Son of God's ministry did not change human nature. The story goes on, still featuring consequences of the Fall. Just as earlier generations had rejected the Torah and the prophets, Jesus' generation rejected him. His crucifixion was interpreted through Isaiah's vision of the "suffering servant": "He was wounded for our transgressions, crushed for our iniquities…upon him was the punishment that made us whole, by his bruises we are healed." (Isaiah 53:5) As Paul wrote to the Corinthians, "…in Christ, God was reconciling the world to himself, not counting their trespasses against them, and entrusting the message of reconciliation to us." (II Corinthians 5:19b) He died for our sins.

Colin Williams explains in a nutshell that "just as Wesley places great stress on the doctrine of original sin in order to make clear that it is only by God's grace that we can be saved, so he places his central emphasis on the Atonement to make it clear that it is only at great cost that God has provided the grace by which we can be forgiven."[1] This Jesus accomplished on the Cross.

Wesley concludes, "This therefore is the general ground of the

whole doctrine of justification."[2] Scholars call the foregoing the "meta-narrative." A good everyday word is that this is our Christian "big Story" within which we find our own salvation journey.

The Theology of Infant Baptism

Many children of Methodist homes begin their journey at the initiative of their parents and in recognition of God's "preparing grace." That is, we are baptized as infants. In Wesley's England, all children were baptized in the Anglican Church. As Wesley led the Revival and saw thousands of others coming to personal faith, he addressed the sacrament of Baptism only once — the publication of one of his father's treatises: on Christian Baptism, which re-stated the orthodox Anglican position — that baptism carries with it 'regenerating grace.' According to Albert Outler, Wesley by the 1760's had moved away from his earlier belief in baptismal regeneration and preached the necessity of a new birth.

In America, the norm for coming to faith was conversion, not baptism. Indeed, Methodist preachers and exhorters were forbidden to baptize because until 1784, none was ordained. During the generation when Methodism was becoming the largest religious organization in America, "preaching and singing" pre-empted the sacraments. Most converts were youth or adults. Most had not been baptized as infants. On the frontier after 1784 when The Methodist Episcopal Church was officially "born," baptism followed conversion. The mode was optional — sprinkling, pouring, or immersion.

Baptism of infants was called "Christening" and was not at all universal until well into the 20th century. The theology of infant baptism was interpreted as a celebration of God's prevenient or "preparing" grace, not regeneration. Under the nurturing influence of parents and the church, upon reaching the "age of accountability," youth were urged to "profess Christ as personal savior." The "age of accountability" was usually about age twelve, but it varied greatly from family to family and preacher to preacher. Unbaptized youth and adults were also urged to repent and accept Christ as personal savior and Lord of their lives for further growth in grace. As William Sangster of British Methodism wrote, "In the eighteenth and early nineteenth centuries, it was generally understood that a Methodist Church was a place where one went to get one's soul saved."[3]

As more and more whole families became converted, children were reared in a Christian home. Catechisms and class meetings were replaced by Sunday School. By the 1850's, the revival fires were ebbing. The revival as a paradigm for "radical outreach" was over. In the 20th century, they were almost banked except as annual ritual by Methodist pastors of evangelical bent.

Writing in 1924 Gilbert Rowe of Duke Divinity School insisted, "Whatever significance baptism may have, it cannot change the quality of the soul. If that which is born of flesh is flesh, and that which is born of spirit is spirit; then that which is born of water is water. Baptism and Holy Communion are means of grace, but the only hope for the individual and the world is in the spirit of Jesus Christ."[4] Written in 1926 and reflecting Methodism then, this statement would still be embraced among neo-evangelicals. Among most United Methodist clergy, it would not! We report; you decide!

By the 1970's United Methodism's major theological voices were resurrecting Wesley's aforementioned *A Treatise on Baptism* from his father's papers. The paper endorsed what is known as "baptismal regeneration." In this theology, a child becomes a Christian with the Sacrament of Baptism. Embracing this sacramentalist view of coming to faith has become the interpretation nearest an "official position" in United Methodism. It represents a major shift from historical Wesleyan theology, and a major departure from the "conversion" theology of our earlier years.

The late 19th century was also the time that Methodism quietly laid Wesley's sermons and spiritual journey aside. Most who felt called to teach went to Europe for their theological training who mentors who "knew not Wesley." By the 1940's, most Methodist seminaries required only one course in "Methodism" during the whole three years and nine academic hours leading to a degree and ordination. The word "Arminianism" was lost and Wesley was reduced to a few sayings.

A Glance at "Coming to Faith" — "then and now"

In 18th century England, virtually everyone had been baptized at birth in the Anglican or Catholic Church. Therefore, Wesley did not include baptism when he listed the "means of grace." Indeed his own baptism did not satisfy his spiritual need for the inner peace of "blessed assurance" even though he had been baptized for thirty-five years and ordained for thirteen! Whatever the grace in the sacrament of baptism, it was "sinned away" by Wesley and, he taught, by everyone. He had practiced the **"faith of a dutiful servant"** before his "strangely warming" experience of grace on May 24, 1738 at the Moravian meeting on Aldersgate Street in London, On that night of his long and faithful journey, he came into the relationship of **"faith of a son**." The Holy Spirit witnessed to Wesley's spirit that he was a child of God, and in Paul's words, "If a child, then an heir, and heir of God and a joint heir with Christ." We argue as to which label to put on his experience of grace at Aldersgate, but in the words of Rupert Davies, "Psychologically it was a complete turning point in the life of John Wesley. Until now, his immense spiritual and mental energies had been mostly directed upon himself…brooding over the state of his soul and trying to improve it. Now those energies were released, and immediately directed outward to those of his fellow men who stood in need of the same liberation as he himself had received. Theologically, Aldersgate was no less important. He had obeyed a 'serious call to holiness' since college, indeed obeyed it to the limits of his power and will. Through Moravian mentor Peter Bohler, Wesley realized he had omitted one vital stage on the way to holiness—faith in Christ as one's personal savior! Without that, it is useless to try to be holy."[5]

From a "conversion" Theology to "gradualism"

Actually a different journey to faith began in Methodism as long ago as the 1880's. Methodist Sunday School literature began to emphasize the "stories" of the Old and New Testaments and almost censored any references to the Cross and experiential conversion. The philosophy of the religious education movement replaced conversion with "gradualism." Fewer Methodists could cite a time and place of conversion. "Church-ianity" unwittingly replaced "Christ-ianity."

As Sunday School declined by the 1960's, **confirmation classes** became the major means of bringing children to personal faith and/or church membership. In confirmation, most emphasis was placed on history, creeds, worship, and membership vows rather than the Wesleyan "way of salvation" which we elicit from Wesley's sermons. We had "slip-slided" our way from the experiential grace confirmed by a "witness of the Spirit with our spirit that we are children of God" (Romans 8:16) of early Methodism to decision confirmed by attending a class.

Revival theology experienced a popularist movement comeback with the ministry of Billy Graham who reaches thousands. However, a close study of Graham's "Decisions for Christ" revealed that most who came forward had some previous influence from some church but had strayed. Sadly for Methodism, many new converts with Methodist roots did not "come home" to their childhood churches, but found their new faith communities elsewhere. The music and ethos of Methodism by the mid 20th century lacked the fervor or biblical emphasis of the Graham meetings. A new evangelical style with neo-Calvinist theology and contemporary worship became the feature of the church growth movement.

Beyond Methodism today, a morphed version of revivalism continues in the neo-evangelical and Fundamentalist churches. In worship, conversion usually comes as response to a sermon called for one's being born again by the Spirit and walking down the aisle to accept Christ. Increasingly, conversion occurs in small groups or one-on-one conversations which usually ask a series of "belief questions" followed by the "sinner's prayer" of confession and repentance. This then becomes the seeker's identifiable moment of being saved. Once it was accompanied by much emotion, but in the churches who still follow this means of evangelization, it is often limited to a handshake and an affirmative, "Brother (sister) you are saved." Today, the Southern Baptist Churches often baptize and receive into membership children as young as age six! Campus evangelical group leaders tend to dismiss totally any means of coming to Christ except via the formula in which they are well versed.

This history will refresh your memory of "how we got where we are." The world changed and we changed, but with less acumen or passion for saving souls. We are threatened with have been shuffled from being "mainline" to being "sidelined." Sadly, we are reaching very few of the "last, the least and the lost," even among families with Wesleyan heritage. Today, very few people whose lives are "wrecked by sin and shame" come to Christ through our local United Methodist churches. Therefore, it is appropriate that we enunciate the "Methodist fundamentals" of coming to faith, or what Wesley called the "way of salvation."

Wesley's Understanding of becoming a Christian

Without question, Methodism through the 19th century was not a liturgical church nor did its theology lean toward Anglican "sacramentalism" until the late 20th century. Through most of our history, Wesley's experience at Aldersgate has been seen in the way it is defined by Rupert Davies, late Methodist theologian in Great Britain: "When we read that his 'heart was strangely warmed,' we are to understand that the conscious emotion which accompanied the great deliverance was strange to him, for he was not an emotional man. We do not know that this 'strange warmth' ever visited him again; his life thereafter was founded, not on an emotion, but on the gift of God granted to him at that moment and continued to him, with occasional interruptions, through all his remaining days.

Psychologically, there is no doubt that this was a complete turning point in the life of John Wesley. Until now, his immense spiritual and mental energies had been mostly directed upon himself; he had spent innumerable hours…for most of his life, brooding upon the state of his soul and trying to improve it. Now those energies were released, and immediately directed outward to those of his fellow men who stood in need of the same liberation as he had himself received."[6]

In his 1748 sermon, "Marks of The New Birth," Wesley preached:
> Baptism is not the new birth. A person may be 'born of water' and yet not be 'born of the Spirit.' Lean no more on the staff of that broken reed, that you were born again in baptism. Who denies that you were born children of God, but you have become a child of the devil; therefore you must be born again.[7]

Albert Outler wrote, "The fact is that Wesley had changed his views on this point; his evangelical concern was to separate the 'new birth' from all 'external acts' in order to support his newer emphasis on conversion."[8] **As Outler noted, this sermon reflects "revisions of the conventional notions of baptismal regeneration."**

A second sermon on the same subject was preached in 1760 and is entitled simply, "The New Birth." It was printed in five issues of the "Standard Sermons," and was preached in American Methodism as definitive Wesleyan doctrine until rather recently. In this sermon Wesley roared:
> Was you devoted to God at eight days old and…was you consecrated to God the Father, the Son, and the Holy Ghost? You have defied your baptism a thousand times and you do so still day by day. Be you baptized or unbaptized, you must be born again. Otherwise, it is not possible you should be inwardly holy. Do you say, 'But I attend all the ordinances of God; I keep to my church and sacrament.' It is well you do. But all this will not keep you from hell except you be born again. Go to church twice a day, go to the Lord's table every week, say ever so many prayers in private, hear ever so many sermons…the best that were ever preached; read ever so many good books — still you

must be born again. None of these things will stand in the place of the new birth.[9]

To be faithful to the premise of this book, we must reflect on Wesley's "way of salvation." Therefore, we hope the following can be a means of bringing persons to faith in Christ. The following reflects Wesley's "way of salvation":

A. The Awakening of the soul. George Hunter helped us all in pointing out that the purpose of Wesley's outdoor sermons was very different from the American revival meeting. **Wesley preached for an "awakening of the soul."** In his sermon *The Spirit of Bondage and Adoption*, Wesley preaches, "…by his Word applied with the demonstration of his Spirit, God touches the heart of him that lay asleep in darkness and in the shadow of death. He is shaken out of his sleep and awakes into a consciousness of his danger. Perhaps in a moment, perhaps by degrees, the eyes of his understanding are opened, and now discern the real state he is in." His effort was to sensitize the person "dead in his sins" to the "whisper in the heart" of the Holy Spirit. He considered this the work of the Holy Spirit: "No one can say 'Jesus is Lord' except through the Holy Spirit."

William Abraham puts it this way: "At some point the individual must see what is at stake and look to God for forgiveness; God alone can supply relief to the soul. Coming to faith is not so much making a decision as it is waiting for God."[10] At some point in our lives, through natural conscience or invitational preaching, or a campfire, or a conversation of what Wesley called "holy conferencing," or a small group in a college dorm, or walking in the woods, we get "under conviction" of our sinfulness. We believe that it is God's purpose for every life that we come to saving faith. We categorically do not believe that some are "elected," leaving others to be on the outside of grace. Charles Wesley taught this universal grace through a hymn:

> "Come sinners to the gospel feast;
> let every soul be Jesus' guest
> Ye need not one be left behind;

for God hath bidden all mankind"

Here we differ from the Calvinists who insist that when God elects to save us, grace is irresistible. Wesley considered the crowning dimension of being made the image of God to be "human liberty." We are not marionettes on the end of a string, nor pre-programmed computer chips; we are free moral agents.

Wesley speaks of...one who feels the burden he cannot shake off; who pants after liberty, power and love, but is in fear and bondage still! Then God answers the wretched man crying out, Who will deliver me from this bondage of sin...? We are then, as Wesley puts it "not far from the Kingdom of God."

B. Personal response. Grace now becomes "co-operant," whether we are a child in confirmation class, a student, a young adult, a church member who lacks "blessed assurance," or a prisoner on death row as a serial killer.

At this point, we "activate" the role of the seeker—the human response to God's grace. That is, once our soul is awakened and we are "under conviction" and convinced of our need for outside help, we can "call upon the name of the Lord." Randy Maddox aptly calls this "responsible grace."

A crisis moment comes, either unexpectedly or over a period of many years. We can resist God's gracious offer of salvation, like Governor Felix, whose response was "On some more convenient day on thee I'll call." (Acts 24:25) From that verse came an old gospel hymn, filled with pathos, "Almost persuaded... almost but lost."

On the other hand, we can say, "yes." We, like the prodigal son in Jesus' parable, can "come to ourselves" and "rise and go to our Father." We do not have to stay in the pigsty.

Wesley preached in the sermon "The Spirit of Bondage and Adoption:"
"Then it is that this miserable bondage ends, and he is

no more 'under the law' but under grace. His eyes are opened to see a loving, gracious God. He hears a voice in his inmost soul."[11] of as the Holy Spirit. Given the power of sin over us, only God can save us. Wesley used the metaphor of "porch" to describe this convicting work of prevenient grace, taking us to repentance at the threshold of saving grace.

This means a voluntary acceptance of God's saving grace. We are moved to repent and trust in God's love to, in the words of John the Elder, "cleanse us from all unrighteousness." With all Protestants, Methodists turn to Ephesians 2:8-10: "For by (God's) grace you have been saved through (your) faith; it is a gift of God, not of works so that anyone may boast." Our sins are forgiven.

Entering the "threshold of saving grace" is not a "cookie cutter" process that is the same for everyone. Simplistic approaches such as "Four Spiritual Laws" or praying "the sinner's prayer" assume that "one size fits all," but if we look at Jesus' conversations with different persons, we find that he meets them where they are, adroitly addresses their point of need or their blind spot, and initiates a saving, restorative, healing relationship. Some of us accepted Jesus as children with little more catharsis than the song, "Into my heart, into my heart, come into my heart, Lord Jesus." Our conversion is like the opening bud on a flower or a rising sun. Others of us describe our homecoming to God as "O happy day that fixed my choice."

Harry Emerson Fosdick, long time pastor of Riverside Church in New York City, defined becoming a Christian as "like crossing a river — near the head of the stream where it requires only a small step across a brook, or at the mouth where it requires a long and arduous swim!" Because of the difference in life ages and stages when we come to Christ, our experience of converting grace is different with each person. We must guard against a lockstep process and remember that Jesus met each person in accordance with her or his personality, life situation, and acute need.

C. Repentance. Wesley insists that we must repent before we can have what he called a "heartfelt religion." Repentance is different from remorse. Remorse is a passive feeling of being sorry. It can lead to depression, despondency, and despair. It is a "woe is me" feeling of inescapable guilt. For Wesley, this is the consequence of the convicting work of prevenient grace — "a thorough conviction of sin." It is divinely initiated.

Repentance, in Greek, is, on the other hand, the proactive word *metanoia*, which loosely translated means, "turning around and going the other way." Repentance involves change — in behavior, attitude, and habits of dependency and dysfunctional relationships. The knotty tangle of sin and guilt can be untied only by "internalizing the external We must be cut off from dependency upon ourselves before we can truly depend on Christ. Wesley considered repentance as "an entire change of heart and life." Namely, repentance is a cathartic interaction of our concession with the Holy Spirit's empowering grace so that we can "rise up and walk." **This is the threshold of experiential grace.**

We must emphasize that some clergy and theologians mistakenly attach a doctrinal "litmus paper" test to repentance — a list of sectarian doctrines we must believe. Jesus had no such test for the thief on the cross nor any other person whom I can find in conversation with our Lord! No, repentance is a condition of the heart, not an examination in doctrine. Wesley called this "experimental divinity."

One aspect of repentance which we will come to in the last chapter of this book is that **repentance is necessarily a recurring experience**. An important insight of human nature is reflected in an oft-sung hymn: "Prone to wander, Lord I feel it; prone to leave the God I love." The devil never sleeps! Sometimes we backslide suddenly and precipitously. More often we sin little by little and step by step. The word in older generations was "backslide." The word for drug addicts trying to be clean is "relapse." In my own childhood memory of rough and ready people coming to a new experience of saving faith, their weekly testimony was, "Pray for me that I will hold out faithful." The syntax of their grammar was poor, but their recognition of the seductive allure of temptation was real.

D. Faith. In Jesus ministry, he met people where they were and treating each of them uniquely. In this age of the Spirit, the Holy Spirit meets us where we are. We can be of any age, ethnicity, disposition or religious heritage. Once again, we must insist on allowing the Holy Spirit freedom from any lockstep patterns or hidden motivational persuaders. However, whatever the setting and circumstance, some things are critical to maintain integrity. This is more than "membership training" in church membership, more than believing that the Bible is the Word of God and that Jesus died on the cross for our sins and that we are penitent.

Faith, in Wesley's language is, "a sure trust and confidence that Christ died for my sins, that God loves me." We must remember that for Wesley, God's "way of salvation" is anchored in God's character—love. In order to trust him, we must internalize this and it is hard to do!"[12]

William Paul Young in *The Shack* has God saying to Mack who cannot move from repentance to faith:
> The real underlying flaw in your life, Mackenzie, is that you don't think I am good. If you knew I was good and that everything — the means, the ends, and all the processing of individual life events — is all covered by my goodness, **then while you might not always understand what I am doing, you would trust me**. You cannot produce trust just like you cannot 'do' humility…. **Trust is the fruit of a relationship in which you know you are loved. Until you know I love you, you cannot trust me.**[13]

A major roadblock in trusting God and having faith in just what William Younger said — a question about the character of God's goodness and love. As Steve Harper points out, it was the "prodigal son's trust in his father's love that gave him the confidence to go home."[14] Sadly, the Calvinist and cultural theology have made us believe in God's sovereignty and power as dominating God's nature.

The foundational Methodist fundamental is that God's dominant attribute is love. If we believe God is love, then we can fall into God's arms of mercy and pardon and "hear" Jesus' words, "Come to me all you who labor and are burdened, and I will give you rest. For my yoke is easy and my burden is light." When our seeking soul is honest with God, we encounter a mystery — God's grace gives the seeker the ability to respond.

Wesley preached "The Circumcision of the Heart" — what Outler calls a "landmark sermon" — in 1733 at Oxford and in revised form just after Aldersgate. Wesley said,

"The best guide of the blind, the surest light of them that are in darkness, the most perfect instructor of the foolish is faith. All things are possible to him who thus believeth, the eyes of his understanding being enlightened, he sees what is his calling, even to glorify God."

He repeats the "faith as revealed in scripture"; then adds, but likewise the revelation of Christ's unmerited love to me a sinner, assures a confidence in His pardoning mercy, wrought in us by the Holy Spirit — a confidence whereby every true believer is enabled to bear witness, "I know that my Redeemer liveth... I know he loved me and gave himself for me." [15]

Faith is more than doctrinal belief; it is a heartfelt trust in God. William Abraham wrote, **"Vague faith in God as creator will not cut it. Nor will bare assent to the creed of the church be enough."**[16] The vows of church membership do not equate faith in Christ. Nor is a series of ethical and moral decisions based on "What Would Jesus Do?" sufficient. To be meaningful, this moment must be deeply personal. I call it a God-moment: the deep reached by the Deep! This is similar to Wesley's experience at Aldersgate — to trust in God's love and make the leap of faith, really a surrendering of one's will to the will of God.

Charlotte Elliott was an invalid who was bitter to the point that no nurse could care for her very long. Then she made this leap of faith and wrote about it in lyrics that have called millions to a similar experience:

> "Just as I am thou wilt receive,
> Will welcome, pardon, cleanse, relieve.
> Because thy promise I believe,
> O Lamb of God, I come, I come."

When a seeker comes to faith, if they have been baptized in a Methodist, EUB, or any other Christian church, we affirm the authenticity of that baptism. If they have not been baptized, the *Book of Discipline* requires us to **offer them the sacrament by either mode—sprinkling, pouring, or immersion**. All modes of baptism are authentic and all have some scriptural basis.

Questions for Reflection or Discussion

1. This chapter is crucial to anyone's faith journey who is a seeker or who is questioning her/his faith experience. Did you find it helpful? Could you lift this chapter alone out of this book and give it to someone giving evidence that their "soul is being awakened"?

2. The biggest controversy of doctrine in United Methodism today is about the meaning of baptism. Discuss the baptism of an infant—to you or your small group, is this the moment we become a Christian?

3. Can you personally say, "I have been born again"? (*Do not take this to mean you have to point to a moment or place; note the sentence that our new birth can be like the unfolding of a flower bud or the rising of the sun.*)

4. Do you think everyone at one time or another feels the "whisper of the Holy Spirit" that can lead to an "awakening of the soul," as Wesley called it. Have you had such moments?

5. Think about or discuss some differing paths on which we come to our personal faith.

6. Did you note the difference between remorse and repentance?

7. Do you believe we can backslide? If so, you are not a Calvinist!

8. Do you believe God's saving grace is for all and we can accept or reject it? *If so, you are not a Calvinist!*

"I contend that there is in every believer both the testimony of God's Spirit, and the testimony of his own, that he is a child of God." "The witness of the Spirit bears witness with our Spirit that we are children of God." (Romans 8:16)

—Sermon *"The Witness of the Spirit I"* (1746)

"None who believes the Scripture as the Word of God can doubt the importance of such a truth as this....If we deny it, there is a danger lest our religion degenerate into mere formality.... If we allow it, but do not understand what we allow, we are liable to run into all the wildness of enthusiasm."

—Sermon *"The Witness of the Spirit I"* (1746)

"It more clearly concerns the Methodists, so called, clearly to understand, explain, and defend this doctrine, because it is one grant part of the testimony which God has given them in searching the Scriptures, confirmed in the experience of his children, that this great evangelical truth has been recovered, which had been for many years well nigh lost and forgotten."

—The Witness of the Spirit II (1767)

"I observed many years ago: 'It is hard to find in the language of men to explain the deep things of God....But perhaps one might say by the "testimony of the Spirit" I mean an impression on the soul...."

—The Witness of the Spirit II (1767)

"Let none ever presume to rest any testimony of the Spirit which is separate from the fruit of it. ...the immediate consequence will be the fruit of the Spirit—love, joy, peace, long-suffering, gentleness, goodness, fidelity, meekness, temperance."

—The Witness of the Spirit II (1767)

"If we are wise, we will continually be crying to God until his Spirit cry in our heart, 'Abba, Father.'"

—The Witness of the Spirit II (1767)

"And the outward fruits are doing good to all men, doing no evil to any, and walking in the light...."

—The Witness of the Spirit II (1767)

CHAPTER 7: Fundamental #6
We Can "Know" Our Sins Forgiven

"All who are led by the Spirit of God are children of God. When we cry, 'Abba,' 'Papá,' it is that very Spirit bearing witness with our spirit that we are children of God."

—Romans 8:14, 15b-16

A defining characteristic of Wesleyan faith is called either "witness of the Spirit" or "assurance." Wesley preached two sermons on this, both on the same text and with the same title! He cites the doctrine as a Methodist fundamental by saying, "it more clearly concerns the Methodists...clearly to understand, explain, and defend this doctrine because it is one grand part of the testimony which God has given them to bear to all mankind." It is by his peculiar blessing upon them in searching the Scriptures, confirmed by the experience of his children, that this great evangelical truth has been recovered, which had been for many years well nigh lost and forgotten.[1] Randy Maddox insists that "adoption" is the internalizing of Christianity's central goal: "restoring the due relations between God and humanity by uniting forever the tender Father and the grateful, obedient child."[2]

John and Charles Wesley had their critics about their conviction that we can "know our sins forgiven." In his two sermons "Witness of the Spirit I & II," he uses three arguments to defend the doctrine, "witness of the Spirit":

A. The scriptural foundation is primary, particularly Paul's words on which the sermons are based. Wesley considers this an objective foundation for the "witness of the Spirit" or "blessed assurance":

All who are led by the Spirit of God are the children of

God. For you did not receive the spirit of fear, but you have received the spirit of adoption. When we cry, 'Abba, Father' it is that very Spirit bearing witness with our spirit that we are children of God, and if children, then heirs, heirs of God and joint heirs with Christ (Romans 8:14-17a)

B. The philosophical foundation for the doctrine is sheer logic: this witness must come before "holiness of life and heart"; 1) we must love God before we can be holy; 2) we cannot love God before we know God loves us; 3) we cannot know God's love until his Spirit bears witness with our spirit. Thus, logically, the foundation for our "house of faith" is laid in Romans 8:16! *(Wesley knew this from his own spiritual journey; he had tried the "holy man" route and found himself still "under the law" of measuring up!)*

C. The subjective foundation for the "testimony of the Spirit" is, in Wesley's words, "hard to find in the language of men."
> He sees this witness as one of the "deep things of God." "I mean an inward impression of the soul, whereby the Spirit of God immediately and directly witnesses to my spirit that I am a child of God, that 'Jesus Christ hath loved me and given himself for me,' that all my sins are blotted out, and I, even I, am reconciled to God."[3]

Charles Wesley, as was his custom, converted his brother's prose to verse: How can a sinner know his sins on earth forgiven?
> How can my gracious Savior show
> my name inscribed in heaven?
> What we have felt and seen with confidence we tell
> And publish to the ends of earth the signs infallible!
> We by his Spirit prove and know the things of God,
> The things which freely of his love
> he hath on us bestowed.
> Our nature's turned, our mind transformed
> in all its powers,
> And both the witnesses are joined—
> The Spirit of God with ours.

The context of Aldersgate is important. Wesley had long been dissatisfied with his lack of "assurance of faith." He felt a failure in his short stint as a pastor in Wroote, and his missionary work in Georgia was conflicted to the point he broke contract and returned in February 1738 to London. He preached in four Anglican churches that spring, only to be told that the vestry did not want him to preach for them again! He walked forty-three miles with Peter Bohler, the Moravian who was en route from Germany to Georgia with a layover in England. Bohler said, "My brother, my brother, that philosophy of your must be purged away."[4]

"Assurance" or "witness of the Spirit" was the missing dimension of John Wesley's spiritual journey before Aldersgate. Until this time, his energies were focused on himself; after this time, his energies were focused on bringing others into the Kingdom. In Georgia as a missionary for seventeen months, he worked very hard but his ministry showed little fruit. Furthermore, he had a disastrous romance, and even his regular meetings with the Moravians did not result in "the peace of God which passes our understanding." He left Savannah incognito following evensong in December, 1737. Debarking from Charleston, he left American waters on Christmas Eve! In the winter and spring of 1738, he was burned out, depressed, and saw no professional future as an Anglican priest.

John Wesley was a consecrated man before May 24, 1738. Indeed, he was a holy man, but he was not a happy man. For over three years, he had seen in the German Moravians something he lacked – the quiet confidence of "knowing" one's sins forgiven. Under the mentoring of Moravian Peter Bohler, Wesley had a defining moment in his spiritual journey. In his words:

> About a quarter before nine as one was reading Luther's preface to Romans where he was describing the change which God works in the heart through faith in Christ, I felt my heart strangely warmed. I felt I did trust in Christ, Christ alone, for salvation, and an assurance was given me that He had taken away my sins, even mine, and saved me from the law of sin and death.[5]

Every seeker of experiential grace needs to know that Wesley's long and arduous chapter of faithfulness and near-monastic life style did not bring him what his father Samuel called the "greatest proof of Christianity" — the inward witness. Many a faithful pastor and layperson who has been to church for many years and lived a life of impeccable character and careful morality could say with Wesley that "one thing I lack"— the assurance that my sins are forgiven and that "I know the things of God."

Some of us are like John Wesley, in that we spend our childhood in a Christian family and a warm, loving local church, are confirmed at about age twelve, and will always answer in the affirmative if someone asks, "Are you a Christian?" Like Wesley, we live with high standards of morality, ethics, and self-control of what he called "our tempers." And yet we can lack "knowing God" as he experienced at Aldersgate. We can be a good person, serve on lots of church committees, sing in the choir, and rear a solid family but still have this gnawing emptiness about "converting grace." If this is our sacred journey, we need to take Wesley's advice and "cry out to God" for what Fanny Crosby described as, "Blessed assurance, Jesus is mine / Oh, what a foretaste of glory divine."

Emotions are slippery. In seminary, I took heart at Wesley's words:
> There may be foretastes of joy, peace, and love — and those not delusive, but really from God — long before we have the witness in ourselves, before the Spirit of God witnesses with our spirits that we have . . . forgiveness of sins . . . But it is by no means advisable to rest here. Continue crying to God until his Spirit cry in our heart, 'Abba, Father.' This is the privilege of all children of God.[6]

Professor William Abraham's words speak for most interpreters of Aldersgate: "Wesley had met God for himself. By 1739 he was beginning to integrate all that he had learned and experienced into a new vision of the Christian tradition."[7] From that, all Methodists take our own cue for our spiritual journey. Our "Aldersgate" often comes after many years of faithful discipleship. We do not have a

"God moment" every day or week or month or year. However, when we do, we have a "confidence to tell." Jesus' most common invitation was simple and unexplored: "Follow me." His assuring words become our experience of assurance, "Whoever comes will in no way be cast out." Of all the revival sermons I ever heard, no message was so encouraging to me as a young man that the message one morning in a summer camp from John 15, verses 14 and 11: "You are my friends...I have said these things to you that my joy may be in you and that your joy may be complete."

Randy Maddox insists that Wesley's preference for the work of the Spirit is "healing." If we think "therapeutic" rather than "juridical," we can see Jesus as the Great Physician healing the "sin-sick soul and making the wounded whole." In this Wesley reveals his influence from some Eastern Christian (i.e. Orthodox) theology over Augustine and other Western (i.e. Catholic) theologians. They used the language of the Roman Empire and its legacy of law. Wesley, on the other hand, preached that sin is a disease for which only God has the remedy; therefore we are better served to use terms of the clinic rather than the court! Therefore Wesley's desire is for God's grace to empower us with a recovery of the likeness of God. To accomplish this, we need to be freed from the power of sin and empowered by the Presence of God. A corollary of this is the emphasis of God's love more than God's sense of justice. That is, Jesus did not die to "buy" our forgiveness; God first loved us and sent his Son to reconcile us to the Father. In Jesus, and only in Jesus, does anyone see the perfect portrait of God.

This is implicit in the much-debated John 14:6 text, "No one comes to the Father but by me." It does not mean that God does not love every human being equally as his child; rather, it means that no one sees God as "Abba" or "Papa" except through Jesus. To others, God might be creator, judge, and even redeemer, but not relationally intimate! None other that a Christian would sing, "He walks with me and he talks with me and he tells me I am his own." Yes, that refers to Jesus and Mary Magdalene, but the message is universal.

Jesus said, "Whoever has seen me has seen the Father." (John 14:9)
Bottom line — Methodism's way to salvation is paved with LOVE![8]
Being saved is coming home — forgiven, restored, healed, quietly
confidence. The gospel hymn says it well: "His eye is on the sparrow,
and I know he watches me."

Questions for Reflection and Discussion

1. This chapter has presented as accurately as we know one of the major emphases of Wesley and the first century of Methodism. Yet is it difficult to avoid a guilt trip for people who have not had her or his own "Aldersgate." The assurance of God's love and forgiveness is interwoven with our childhood, youth, and adult church life; our emotional disposition; and our self esteem. How important do you feel this is to being a Christian?

2. If you do not yet have this "blessed assurance," do you seek it?

"There is scarce any word in Holy Write which has given more offense than this—Christian perfection. The word 'perfect' is what many cannot bear. The very sound is an abomination to them. Hence some of have advised to lay aside the use of such expression. But are they not found in the oracles of God. Whatever God hath spoke; that we will preach."

—Sermon "Christian Perfection" 1741

Wesley insisted that the Spirit of God does not cease working in us after we have first experience God's saving grace. He used the term often, "grace upon grace."

"God is continually breathing, as it were, upon his soul, and his soul is breathing unto God. Grace is descending into his heart and prayer and praise ascending to heaven. And by this intercourse between God and man, this fellowship with the Father and the Son, as by a kind of spiritual respiration, the life of God in the soul is sustained; and the child of God grows up till he comes to 'full measure of the stature of Christ.'"

—Sermon, "The New Birth" (1760)

In response to an inquiry from (Anglican) Bishop Edward Gibson about Wesley's version of Christian perfection, Wesley said, "I told him without any disguise or reserve what I mean by perfection." To which the bishop responded, "If this be all you mean, publish it to all the world…."

CHAPTER 8: Fundamental #7
Perfecting Grace — One Day at a Time, Dear Jesus

"Everyone who lives on milk being still an infant, is unskilled in the word of righteousness. Solid food is for the mature, for those whose faculties have been trained to distinguish good from evil.

Therefore let us go on to perfection"

—Hebrews 6:1

"Ask and you will receive, so your joy may be complete."

—John 16:24b

Most Christians have never heard the term, "Christian perfection." Yet perfecting grace cannot be omitted as a Methodist fundamental. Wesley called it "the peculiar doctrine committed to our trust." The concept has never been deleted from ordination examination with the question in every branch of Methodism: "Are you going on to perfection?" Wesley wrote less than a year before his death that the people called Methodist "were raised up to proclaim this truth."

Fifteen months after Aldersgate, Wesley is writing about the rest of one's Christian journey beyond accepting Christ as our personal Savior. He calls it "sanctification." Because that term acquired so much moralistic baggage identified with the "holiness code" of the 19th century, we use the participle form — "perfecting grace"— as we endeavor the recovery of this salient Wesleyan doctrine. Of this dimension of one's journey, Wesley wrote, "I believe it to be an inward thing, namely, the life of God in the soul of man, a participation of the divine nature, the mind that was in Christ, or, the renewal of our heart, after the image of Him that created us."[1]

Colin Williams speaks for the majority of serious Wesley scholars when he wrote, "There can be no doubt of the importance of the doctrine of perfection in the history of Methodism."[2] Wesley wrote in his recap of the rise of Methodism, " . . . men are justified before they are sanctified; but still holiness was their point." God then thrust them (*the Methodists*) out, utterly against their will, to raise a holy people Wesley considered his doctrine of Christian perfection the "*grand depositum*" of Methodism.

Bishop Nolan B. Harmon wrote in his classic, *Understanding The Methodist Church*:

> The doctrine of Christian perfection has been the one specific contribution which Methodism has made to the Church universal. In this one doctrine we stand by ourselves and utter a teaching that reaches up fearlessly and touches the very scepter of God's grace. If we can live one day without sin, we can live two, then many. Why not all?[3]

Harry Denman once taught my family at our parsonage breakfast table how he prayed the Lord's Prayer every morning, "… Thy will be done — **in me, in me** — on earth as it is in heaven." To this saintly layman, perfection meant a daily, conscious conformity to the will of God as he understood it. This is much what Wesley meant when he used the term "perfection of the pilgrim." This we today understand in the idiom, "perfecting grace". In Colin Williams' words, "The perfect Christian is holy, not because he has risen to a required moral standard, but because he lives in a state of unbroken fellowship with Christ."[4] In a letter to brother Charles, in 1762, John Wesley says, "By perfection, I mean the humble, gentle, patient love of God and man ruling all the tempers, words and actions, the whole heart and the whole life."

Bishop Earl G. Hunt often told the apocryphal story of the young man who decided to answer negatively when he stood before the annual conference for ordination and was asked, "Are you going on to perfection?" He therefore answered, "NO." A murmur went across the conference, "What would the bishop do?" The wise bishop simply looked at the young rebel and asked, "Then, son, what are you going on to?" There is much truth in this story! Anything short of perfection will be a goal we can reach and either settle for spiritual stagnation even when life is moving on, or we can look down from our pious pedestal in self-righteousness. If Christian perfection is true to its name, a major characteristic will be continuing openness to the Holy Spirit and honest humility.

What Wesley Did Not Mean

But what do we mean by this "second work of grace" that is so central in the grand scheme of Wesley's "experimental divinity"? To be fair and accurate, let us enunciate what Wesley did not mean by Christian perfection:

Christian infallibility. No one possesses absolute knowledge, perfect judgment, consistent performance, or total control of what Wesley called one's "tempers." Wesley called that "angelism," and said he wanted a holiness for real people engaged in real life.

Superiority. Moving deeper into the "mind which was in Christ" must not breed a rank of "first" or "second" levels of status. The effect must be humility, not pride.

Immunity from life's problems. This is a mistake made by those who combined holiness with the charismatic movement of the 1970s and later. Being sick, falling victim to natural law disasters, being wounded or killed in war, being victim to crime, and losing one's job must not be seen as the lack of Christian perfection. It is not, in Steve Harper's words, "vaccination from reality."[5] It is patently not true that "if you have sufficient faith, you will be healed." Christians die at the same degree as everyone else — 100 percent. All those who preach that message end up dying one day, and we trust their death was not caused by a failure of faith.

Instantaneous "faith accompli" One of my teenage memories is hearing people give specific dates for their conversion and their being sanctified. We can certainly have a liberating experience of surrendering to God some habit, relationship, or attitude that has denied the Holy Spirit's empowering us to grow. However, once that block is moved we must "press on to the high calling which is ours in Christ Jesus." The devil is no slacker and we are constantly being tempted in thought, word, and deed.

What Wesley Did Mean

Robert Cushman insisted that neither the Anglican Articles of Religion, nor Martin Luther, nor John Calvin understood perfecting grace as Wesley did.[6] Wesley had found in his own experiences of seeking to be a holy man while in Oxford and Georgia that holiness is not attainable through self-discipline, but finds it given only and entirely as a gift of the Holy Spirit.[7]

In his sermon "On God's Vineyard," Wesley, in Outler's humorous words, "took a swig of triumphalism"[8]:

Who has wrote more ably than Martin Luther on justification by faith alone, and who was more ignorant of sanctification? How many of the Romish writers have wrote strongly and scripturally on sanctification who were entirely unacquainted with justification? But it has pleased God to give the Methodists a full and clear knowledge of each, and the wide difference between them.[9]

There has probably never been a hymnal among Wesleyans that did not include Charles Wesley's classic, "Love Divine, all love excelling." He was clearly speaking of sanctifying grace:

Breathe, oh breathe, thy loving spirit
into every troubled breast,
Let us all in thee inherit,
let us find that second rest.
Take away our bent to sinning,
Alpha and Omega be
End of faith as its beginning,
set our hearts at liberty.

In another hymn, Charles has us sing,

O may Thy love possess me whole, my joy,
my pleasure, and my crown;
Strange fires far from my heart remove;
my every act, word, thought be love!

Wesley's problem was how to define a life of perfection for
"imperfects" like us! We must not look at humankind through rose-
colored glasses, forgetting creaturely limitations on the one hand and
the continuing effects of original sin on the other.

In the historical context of Methodist "experimental divinity," what
we mean by Christian perfection is this — we grow in grace, we draw
"closer to Thee," until except for constant human frailty and cultural
blindness of which we are not conscious, we can live in relational
harmony with God. Is not "growing in the grace and knowledge of
Jesus Christ" a goal common to every Christian tradition?

Wesley searched the scriptures and found the twelfth chapter
of Romans which has been called "the constitution of Christian
living." Outler says, "It is his doctrine of grace carried to its climax,
an idea with radical implications for personal ethics and social
transformation. It involves the believer I an actual and lively
participation in God's own loving business...."[10]

Bishop Harmon and others write categorically, "Wesley never
claimed for himself that he had been 'made perfect,' even as he
preached it as the goal of the journey."[11] Reflecting Wesley's own
caveats, Bishop Harmon wrote, "this experience does not deliver us
from the infirmities, ignorance, and mistakes common to man, nor
from the possibilities of further sin.[12] The Christian is challenged to
"have the mind which was in Christ Jesus" and to respond wholly
to the will of God as we understand it with the result that sin loses
both its grip and its appeal. The Holy Spirit consciously becomes our
spiritual watchdog through which we examine our soul for sins of
thought, word, and deed.

Christian Perfection Across The Years

Yet perfecting grace remains the most ignored or the most debated and divisive of all Methodist fundamentals. Its proponents first married it to Victorian Puritanism and then immersed it in enthusiasm! Outler reflects on this: "This syndrome of self-righteousness amongst the holiness people led the 'mainstream' to throw the Wesleyan baby of true holiness out with the 'second blessing' bath water."[13] Most were considered fanatics to the point that at the General Conference of 1894, the Episcopal Address of the Methodist Episcopal bishops virtually invited those who would "push' holiness to leave. The result was the founding of the Nazarene Church.

The loss was great because mainline Methodism from that point woefully neglected the essence of Wesley's insistence on "holiness of heart and life." Of the several mergers in the 20th century, there was never an overture to bring back to the mother church those who had left because of either racism or holiness. The sad result was that most Methodists never heard of perfecting grace because most pastors would not touch the subject with a ten foot pole.

For generations, sanctification was maligned by its friends and caricatured by its opponents. It was preached as an instant "second work of grace" received by going to the altar in a revival meeting. The preacher said that while in justifying grace our sins were forgiven, we still retained what the old holiness movement called "carnal nature." In sanctification, one would be baptized by the Holy Spirit and purged of this carnal nature so that henceforth the sanctified would be "spirit filled" and "spirit led." Hillary T. Hudson reflects this in his 1882 edition of *The Methodist Armor*:

> Sanctification brings the whole body, heart, spirit, mind, family, property, influence, and intellect into captivity to Christ so the Christ thinks for him, puts the love of God in his heart. The sanctified Christian is unselfish and beneficent, a vessel of Christian love, the mind to reflect the glory of God, and one's property to advance the cause

of God. Throw yourself into the ocean of divine love, and be filled with all the fullness of God.[14]

If all this seems personal, it is! For four of my teenage years, I was told that an emotional experience of being made "perfect" would come as a baptism of the Spirit instantaneously. It did not, even though I sought it honestly. In its place, I followed the legalism of the holiness code. I abstained not only from alcohol and tobacco but also from dancing, playing cards, and going to movies. I skipped social celebrations during high school. Then, like most of my generation, I abandoned the doctrine for many years.

Because of this painful experience with a distorted version of perfecting grace, I have come to embrace a more recent understanding of Christian perfection as deep yearning of my soul. I find inspiration in Psalm 42: "As a deer longs for flowing streams, so my soul longs for you, O God. My soul thirsts for the living God. When shall I come and behold the face of God…by day the Lord extends his steadfast love, and at night his son is with me, a prayer to the God of my life." I do sometimes ask with the psalmist, "Why are you cast down, O my soul, and why are disquieted within me?" But in my older years, I am developing more and more the confidence of the author of Psalm 130: "I wait for the Lord, my soul waits, and in his word I hope; my soul waits for the Lord more than those who watch for the morning." My greatest guides are those to which we turn in the next chapter—spiritual disciplines that Wesley called "means of grace."

In my renewed journey of seeking God's perfecting grace, Brian Wren speaks to me in his hymn:
> This is a day of new beginnings,
> time to remember and move on
> Time to believe what love is bringing,
> Laying to rest the pain that's gone.
> Christ is alive and goes before us
> to show and share what love can do
> This is a day of new beginnings,

our God is making all things new.

Having admitted that both "holiness code" proponents and "modernity" opponents of Christian perfection did us a disservice, **let us renew our insistence that perfecting grace is a Methodist fundamental!** Wesley borrowed from a wide and deep stream of piety in his insistence on a goal of "perfect love" and its two-dimensional focus of "loving God and loving neighbor." He says, "This is the sum of Christian perfection: It is all comprised in that one word, LOVE."[15]

Perfecting grace is our continuing willingness to "let go and let God have his wonderful way" in our lives. An old gospel hymn, "Higher Ground," had the line,

I'm pressing on the upward way, new heights
I'm gaining every day;
Still praying as I'm onward bound,
'Lord plant my feet on higher ground.'
My heart has no desire to stay where
doubts arise and fears dismay;
Tho' some may dwell where these abound,
'Lord plant my feet on higher ground.'[16]

Two nuances of grammar are theologically important. Wesley spoke of "going on" to perfection more than of having arrived. To claim perfection reflects Pharisaism and sanctimonious spiritual pride. The second grammatical nuance is "perfecting grace." This is in keeping with Wesley's description of the Christian journey as "grace upon grace." Perfecting grace is, in Bishop Ken Carder's words, "a gift (of God) emerging from friendship with and obedience to Christ, a process of maturing in discipleship until the heart is habitually inclined to do what is right. Perfection must never be seen as perfectionism."[17]

In teaching seminary students, I employ Wesley's metaphor of "the porch" as God's convicting grace leading us to repentance, "the door" as our co-operant response of accepting God's love and experiencing justifying grace, and "the house" as God's taking us room to room for the rest of our lives. At each room God takes us by the arm and says, "I need to look in this room." We are often resistant and say, "No, Lord, I am not yet ready to let you cleanse and purge that dark stain from my life." Often it is a broken relationship, a nagging guilt, or even a living lie. So God says, "I must go in there. We cannot bypass a skeleton-occupied closet on our way to the pretty parlor." The Holy Spirit continues to whisper to our heart, to nudge our conscience, to lead us to new insights through relationships, readings and means of grace.

Bishop Carder reminds us that justifying grace is what God does *for* us in the effecting of Jesus' death for the forgiveness of sin, and sanctifying grace is what God does *in* us—holiness in life. These do not affirm human potential as much as the power of God."[18] He also points out our tendency to interpret sin through our provincial cultures; thus, we are blinded from "seeing ourselves as others see us" (to quote Robert Burns). Sanctification must be seen from a higher plane than parish, region, nation, race, gender, income, and denomination.

Wesley, to his credit, always insisted that sanctification is "love of God and love of neighbor." Jason Vickers, a young scholar reared in the Nazarene Church's ethos of holiness and now a professor at United Theological Seminary, agrees: "Wesley regarded entire sanctification or Christian perfections as having above all to do with the filling of the human heart with love for God and neighbor and the governing of all subsequent thoughts, words, and deeds, by that love." [19]

Walter Muelder has written, "Twentieth century holiness envisages a whole person in a whole society."[20] Reinhold Niebuhr enlightened us on the difficulty of being a moral individual in a society tainted by sin. Presbyterian Scot John Baille acknowledged that Reformation thought does not take seriously enough the possibility of holiness in Christian living. In the late-twentieth century, Methodism recovered Wesley's insistence on "grace upon grace" or perfecting grace, but we also recovered his insistence that there "is no holiness but social holiness." To grow in grace, to be discipled into the "mind that was in Christ Jesus," Wesley outlined what he called the "means of grace." To those we now turn.

There's one thing every Christian has in common—that Jesus has said, "Follow me."

I love the words of Albert Schweitzer:
> He comes to us . . . just as on the shore of the lake He approached those men who knew him not. His words are the same: 'Follow thou Me!' and He puts us to the tasks He has to carry out in our age. He commands. And to those who obey, be they wise or simple, He will reveal Himself in the fellowship of peace and activity, of struggle and suffering, till they come to know, as an inexpressible secret, Who He is . . .[21]

Kurt Kaiser and Ralph Carmicheal published a gospel song in the sixties that speaks to and for me:
> "I wish for you my friend this happiness that I've found;
> You can depend on God; it matters not where you're bound
> I'll shout it from the mountaintop.
> I want the world to know
> The Lord of love has come to me; I want to pass it on.
>
> Once you've experienced it, you want to sing
> It 's fresh like spring, you want to pass it on."

Questions for Reflection and Discussion

1. Within the Methodist Church have you ever heard taught or preached the "doctrine of sanctification?" Have you heard it in another church during your journey? To you is this a new concept of grace?

2. Did you find this chapter helpful?

2. Do you feel yourself "drawn" to a personal journey of perfecting grace, or does it "put you off"?

3. To either answer, "Why?" What attracts you? What repels you?

4. If you have any desire to "grow in grace", you are now ready to move to the next chapter on Wesley's "means of grace"!

Soon after Wesley's influence by the Moravians and his heart warming experience in a Moravian prayer meeting, Wesley began having conflicts with the Moravians meeting on Fetter Lane in London. They insisted on the doctrine of "stillness," meaning that when you were converted, there were no subsequent "means of grace" except communion with Jesus. By 1746 many Methodists were wanting a complete break with Anglicanism and saw no necessity for what they called "outward observances" in being Christians of the Methodist movement. They considered baptism of infants, Holy Communion, and attendance at Anglican worship as superfluous. Their total emphasis was on their conversion experience and "enthusiasm." Like Luther in the Protestant Reformation two centuries earlier who ransacked all the Catholic Churches and monasteries, Wesley's followers were making everything "spiritual" and nothing to be liturgical, or orderly — private or public.

In a tract, "The Character of a Methodist," he still insisted that our primary call is that through us "the love of God is shed abroad in his heart by the Holy Ghost given unto him."

But the time had come for Wesley to discipline his "adolescent children." His "means of grace" were really reflective of the Book of Common Prayer of his beloved Church of England. He outlined what we know as the "General Rules," which can be summarized, "Do no harm, do all the good you can, and participate in the ordinances of the Church."

A case can be made for the possibility that the means of grace created an unbridgeable chasm between the "quietism" of the Moravians and the "middle way" of the Methodists. Wesley the Anglican could not lead a movement that did not insist on the practical and "observable" spiritual disciplines like Bible study, prayer, the Lord's Supper, and corporate worship. The consequence has been a series of "swings" in Methodist history between a very free spirit of evangelical enthusiasm and a more liturgical, disciplined church order with high appreciation of orderliness and tradition..

If "means" become "ends," they are idolatrous; but without disciplined means, we might well come to sectarian and schismatic "ends." Again, mutual heritage of "strangely warm heart" and means of grace make us a church of the "middle way."

CHAPTER 9: Fundamental #8
Mr. Wesley's "Means of Grace"

"I pray that, according to the riches of his glory, he may grant that you may be strengthened in your inner being with power through the Spirit and that Christ may dwell in your hearts through faith, as you are being rooted and grounded in love."

—Ephesians 3:16-17

"Religion that is pure and undefiled before God, the Father is this: to care for orphans and widows in their distress.... What good is it if you say you have faith but do not have works? Can faith save you? Faith by itself, if it has no works, is dead."

—James 1:27; 2:14, 17

The overall theme of this book is God's grace, but how does God reach us with this grace? I love the words of George Croly, vicar of a small Anglican parish:

"I ask no dream, no prophet ecstasies,No sudden rending
of this veil of clay, No angel visitant, no opening skies.
But take the dimness of my soul away."

Like many of us, Wesley grew up in the church. Like many clergy, he felt God's call to ordained ministry while he was in college. For thirteen years (1725-38), he read deeply in the writings of saints who urged every Christian to be very disciplined, to practice acts of Christian mercy, and certainly to "attend the ordinances of God," by which they meant the various ministries of the local church. During this chapter of his life, he practiced what he always called "holiness of heart and life." In this time of his spiritual journey he lacked the assurance of his personal salvation and the "peace which passes understanding." He came to that experience through the mentoring of the Moravians.

Eighteen months after the Moravians had "midwifed" Wesley's experience of "knowing his sins forgiven" at Aldersgate, he could not longer abide their doctrine of "stillness." They insisted that until a person had "full assurance of faith," they should not take Communion nor practice any works of mercy. Rather they should "lie still at Jesus' feet" until they had an emotionally cleansing experience of faith. By contrast, Wesley would not negate his years of leading the Holy Club at Oxford, where they ministered to prisoners, organized daycare for children, fed the poor, and insisted, "There is no holiness without social holiness." Wesley insisted that Christianity cannot be a "solitary religion." He insisted that ethics is the fruit of faith and he abhorred any doctrine that "allows a believer to have a passive attitude toward either the means of grace or the demand of the Gospel for actual righteousness."[1]

Wesley broke with the Moravians because he insisted that "weak faith" can be strengthened by the means of grace, which the church alone supplies. He said, "I believe it is right for him who knows not faith to go to church, commune, pray, read the Scripture, do all the temporal good he can and endeavour after doing spiritual good..."[2] By the discipline of these means, we are encouraged to pursue the "high calling which is ours in Christ."

By July 20, 1740, the final break came when the Methodists left the Moravians forever. Wesley said conclusively:

> There are means of grace, i.e. outward ordinances, whereby the inward grace of God is ordinarily conveyed to man before the faith that brings salvation ... One of these means is the Lord's Supper. He who has not faith should wait for it through the use of this and other means by which God hath ordained.[3]

Unlike Martin Luther, John Wesley loved the book of James! Methodism has always been known for establishing orphanages, funding missional ministries, founding colleges, sponsoring homes for the mentally challenged, responding to disasters, and ministering with the poor. Therefore Wesley's "means of grace" are the capstone of Methodist fundamentals.

William Abraham helps us clarify that while Wesley's first concern was the salvation of souls, he insisted that God had supplied various means for the reception of grace, and most of those means are standard practices of your local church![4] The reality is that for those of us who grew up in Christian homes, went to Sunday school and church, and made early commitments to Christ, the "means of grace" nurtured us in the faith until we, like Wesley, had our own "Aldersgate" experience. Without the church we would be spiritual orphans.

Fundamentalists often glory in citing a moment of being "saved," as if that is the sum and summary of being a Christian. For Wesley, the moment of what he called "justifying grace" was the threshold of grace, not God's completed work with us. At that point, he said, we are children in the faith, and that "grace reigns, but sin remains."[5] St. Paul compared this stage of being a Christian with that of a baby who could be nourished only on milk, but who needed to grow into a diet which included meat.

We err to make spiritual discipline into a magic mantra! Wesley indeed in his sermon "The Means of Grace" warned:

> Before you use any means let it be deeply impressed on your soul: There is no power in this. It is in itself a poor, dead, empty thing; separate from God, it is a dry leaf, a shadow . . . Settle this in your heart . . . that there is no power to save but in the Spirit of God . . . consequently even what God ordains conveys no grace to the soul if you trust not in him alone.[6]

Then Wesley listed the means by which we can either be led to "the full assurance of our salvation" or that we can be sustained as we walk the road less traveled to grow through the seasons and experiences of life, a journey which Wesley called "grace upon grace." We consider it therefore a Methodist fundamental that these ordinary channels are often the occasions when we have our God moments. They are necessary; we need them. Thomas a Kempis once wrote, "I have never found anyone so religious and devout that he had not sometimes a withdrawing of grace or felt not some decrease of zeal."[7]

In Albert Outler's 1974 Fondren lectures at Southern Methodist University, morphed his lifetime of scholarly Wesleyan study into a rather folksy presentation. In his last lecture, he summarized Wesley's doctrine of holiness with his logic: "We have faith in order to love, we love in order to be good, we are good in order to be happy—all of which is what God made us for in this world and the next. This is 'holy living' as John Wesley saw it."[8]

When Wesley spoke of Christian perfection as a dimension of grace theology, his doctrine was always accompanied by his exhortation to "go on" to perfection. **See the journey imagery!** Let us think of this as a continuing enrichment of internalizing God's love and grace.

John Wesley had been taught from infancy to hold his emotions in check and he consequently was not psychologically given to exuberance, flippancy, or small talk. And yet, according to his admirers and critics, Wesley had a strange, insistent reality of cheerfulness, joy, and high spirits. He was, in Outler's words, "a happy man." Outler identified fifty-four quotes in which Wesley paired "happy" with "holy." He died happy, singing, praying and with the words on his lips, "Best of all, God is with us." We would do well to follow his model of spiritual discipline as a means of conquering many of our human infirmities, channeling our energies into outward works of righteousness, and ending our struggle with unforgiven sins and unresolved guilt.

Millions of nominal Christians who fill the pews and support the church budgets are "salt of the earth" people who have served faithfully on church committees, kept some modicum of our church vows, and practiced morality as a lifestyle. Wesley would disagree with those who negate those years of our spiritual journey when we followed Christ "from a distance." He called this "weak faith" but did not negate it. Wesley said point-blank to the Moravians, "There are degrees of faith. A man may have some degree of it before all things in him are become new—before he has the full assurance of faith, the abiding witness of the Spirit, or the clear perception that Christ dwelleth in him."[9]

In his own sermon, "The Means of Grace," Wesley recognized that the Church had tragically neglected many of the poor, the disenfranchised, and the "quiet of the land" as well as the drunkards, thieves, and rascals! But then he made the case for the "means of grace" as "outward signs, words, or actions ordained of God to be the ordinary channels whereby he might convey to men preventing, justifying, and sanctifying grace."

In frontier American Methodism's sacramental heritage atrophied terribly. The early testimonials are filled with vivid and spontaneous experiences of grace. In recent years, we have moved more to a journey enriched and deepened by Wesley's means of grace. Consequently, in Methodism, we have an interweaving of spiritual discipline and an evangelical experience of God's saving grace. Between the liturgical churches and the evangelistic "free" churches, we are the "church of the middle way."

Using these expressive actions as vehicles for God to convey grace are means by which we respond to God's grace. When a trainer "breaks" a horse, the trainer does not break the horse's will; rather the trainer channels the horse's abilities to a more useful purpose, and indeed, to an almost intimate relationship, as we learn from the techniques of "the horse whisperer." Properly done, the training process fulfills what we understand to be the horse's creative purpose and meaning! It is definitively co-operant and synergistic — the trainer and the horse in mutually responsive relationship. Just so, the undisciplined person might seem to be free, but in reality has no meaning and purpose in life. By God's means of grace, we exchange the heavy yoke of sin for Jesus who said, "My yoke is easy and my burden is light." Discipline is really liberating.

As the late psychologist and author Scott Peck said in the opening line of his book, *The Road Less Traveled*, "Life is difficult." Trouble comes and we need more than the distant memory of Confirmation or conversion to cope with it. Wesley's means of grace provide the Holy Spirit a constant "wave length" through which God's steadying love can carry us through the "treacherous shoals" of life.

If we are to grow in "taming our bears," "caging our lions," and knowing our purpose, we must have some spiritual discipline. We can attain the faithful courage to say "no" to sins of the flesh and sins of the spirit that entice us. We can practice the presence of God and see love overcome fear. We can attain a lifestyle that combines responsibility with freedom and freedom with responsibility. Just as Paul said, "I can do all things through Christ who strengthens me."

Bishop Bevel Jones used to love the doggerel: "The main thing is to keep the main thing the main thing." An old gospel hymn had us sing, "Keep your eyes upon Jesus." Paul urged us to "let the mind be in you which was in Christ Jesus." John Wesley's was a "practical divinity." It was not a pretty world into which Wesley sought to bring some ordering of private lives, some decency in human behavior, some peace to domestic violence, and some growth in personal grace.

Methodism was a movement among the masses — men who drank too much at the pub, women who were shrews, abused children who became abusers when they had children, the world of *Oliver Twist* and *Little Lord Fauntleroy*.

Wesley's converts were no "rope of sand," but a connected, disciplined "order" of bands, class meeting, and societies. In each of them, Methodists were urged to develop the disciplines called "means of grace." The term "means of grace" fell into disuse for many years of Methodist preaching and teaching. For Wesley, these "means" were not ends in themselves, but were tutors, or spiritual disciplines. He insisted that they can be God's means of leading us from what he called "weak faith" to a mature relationship with God in all the dimensions of our lives — habits, attitudes, relationships, and spiritual disciplines.

Therefore, I encourage you, dear reader, whatever your age, life stage or psychological disposition to practice Wesley's means of grace. Do not fall prey to the cultural mythology that "being spiritual" will make you morbid or a wimp. Christian discipleship empowers us with faithful courage.

Wesley's Means of Grace

"By 'means of grace' I understand outward signs, words, or actions, ordained of God to be ordinary channels whereby

He might convey to men, preventing, justifying, and sanctifying grace."[10]

—John Wesley, 1741

#1: Prayer, whether in secret or the great congregation

I love the concept of prayer in James Montgomery's (1818) words:
"Prayer is the soul's sincere desire, unuttered or expressed,"
The motion of a hidden fire that trembles in the breast.
Pray is the burden of a sign, the falling of a tear,
The upward glancing of an eye, when none but God is near."[11]

Our prayer life is often so "catch as catch can" that we must with Jesus disciples of old request today, "Lord, teach us how to pray."

Let us practice beginning our prayers with meditation on a recent scene of beauty in creation, or the music of a great choir, or some other reminder of God's majesty. I begin often with Psalm 103: "Bless the Lord, O my soul, and all that is within me, bless your Holy Name." This moves us out of our own little world and mentally into the presence of the Creator. Then, unless we are in a crisis moment, let us be careful to "count our blessings" before we move to our burdens. Giving thanks for what is gives us an "attitude of gratitude." It at least balances our complaining about what is not.

Naturally, we are going to ask for God to help us in our life situation, but prayers of petition must not monopolize our prayers, making of the Lord God Almighty our personal errand boy. Intercessory prayers are powerful; they give God a chance to call us to be the "loving heart" or the "act of kindness" that is needed by the person or situation for which we are praying. Our motive is concern, not ordering the Almighty to do his homework! We must caution against being too casual with our promise, "I'll pray for you." They may need a hug or a phone call or card or a sandwich for their next meal. We can so easily make a casual promise to pray for someone and simply forget that we have committed ourselves to the sacred covenant of intercessory prayer.

Lastly, we need to do our own spiritual housecleaning, asking God to empower us to do what we cannot do alone—to forgive, to have faithful courage, to overcome fear, to "kick" habits, and to trust God as one who loves us.

Because I am a person afflicted with insomnia, I close my nighttime prayer by asking for release from the burdens and stress of the day followed by a slow, meditative recitation of the 23rd Psalm. At the lowest moment of my life, in the winter of 1980, I had a "God moment" as the sun was rising over Kansas City, and I reached that long familiar line: "He maketh me to lie down in green pastures." I had always concentrated on the green pastures and skipped the predicate! That night/morning I realized that sometimes because God loves us, God has to discipline us. I had to be made to lie down before I could get Don out of the driver's seat, and look up to God as the "rod and staff" who would lead me through the valley, deliver me from fear of evil, fill my cup, and anoint my head with the "balm of Gilead" that "makes the wounded whole and cures the sin-sick soul." The 23rd Psalm is my guide into God's will, followed by God's promises.

Another dimension of prayer that has become increasingly meaningful for me is the rich mine of prayers and hymns from the Church across the ages. I have sprinkled hymn quotes throughout this book. I mention here only two prayers. One is a prayer that was in the older Lord's Supper liturgy of The Methodist Church—the "Prayer of Humble Access." The essence of this prayer is:

"We do not presume to come . . . trusting in our own righteousness but in Thy manifold and great mercies. We are not worthy so much as to gather up the crumbs under Thy table, but Thou are the same Lord whose nature is always to have mercy. . . "

The other is the "Collect for Purity":

"Almighty God, unto whom all hearts are open, all desires known, and from whom no secrets are hid; cleanse the thoughts of our hearts by the inspiration of Thy Holy Spirit, that we may perfectly love Thee and worthily magnify Thy Holy Name."

These prayers I have long ago committed to memory and find more helpful in many life situations that to coin my own verbiage in talking with my Father who art in heaven.

#2: Search the Scriptures

Paul wrote to young Timothy, "All scripture is inspired . . . for training in righteousness" (I Timothy 3:16). The sense of the term "means of grace" is certainly implied in this text. The saddest plight of spiritual poverty for most Christians is biblical illiteracy. The reason we so easily fall prey to false doctrines is that people manipulate the scriptures and play biblical hopscotch, and we have not mastered the Bible enough to counter those who confuse us.

Before we can properly hear God's word, verse by verse, we need to learn what is called the "meta-narrative" or the "macro" view of the whole of scripture. In essence, Wesley advised us to take the "micro" texts and project them onto the "macro" biblical message. If they do not seem to fit, determine if the text "computes" with the larger message of the Bible and especially of Jesus.

Article of Religion #V reads, " The Holy Scriptures containeth all things necessary for salvation." Note the difference in this 16th century definition of scripture and the Fundamentalist insistence on "plenary inspiration" that was first circulated in 1918. The Bible is the Word of God, inspired in its writing and intended for "reproof, correction, and training in righteousness." (II Timothy 3:16)

We must search the Scriptures for language, cultural context, theological context, and style of literature, but we must never lose sight of Scripture as the Word of God, holistically and redemptively. With all the good benefits of biblical criticism since the mid-19th century, scholars have often dissected the Bible and never put it together again! That is like a surgeon who would remove our organs for examining, then not put us together again!

Charles Wesley is our best teacher here:
>Whether the Word be preached or read,
>no saving benefit I gain
>From empty sounds or letters dead,
>unprofitable all and vain
>Unless by faith thy word I hear
>and see its heavenly character.
>If God enlighten through his Word,
>I shall my kind Enlightener bless;
>But void and naked of my Lord,
>what are all verbal promises?
>Nothing to me, till faith divine,
>inspire, inspeak, and make them mine.[12]

Searching the Scripture is different from academic Bible study or sermon preparation. We need first to do our study, learning all we can from commentators. Commentators who reflect their knowledge of Hebrew and Greek, archeology, and culture can bring much light to a text that I would never know without their help. If possible, compare more than one translation and version. The "NIV" is an excellent translation reflecting conservative scholarship and the

"NRSV" is equally excellent, reflecting a more liberal theology where there is question about Hebrew or Greek phrases. We should, in 2011, buy the *Common English Bible*, being published on the 400th anniversary of that "noblest monument of English prose," the King James Version. I love to check even para-phrased Bibles, especially Eugene Peterson's *The Message*.

To "search the Scripture," we must have the Bible, or Bibles, and a place of meditation and focus. We are not "strip mining"; we are "deep drilling." Read it slowly, sometimes word by word. Stop and meditate on its meaning. Read it aloud if possible. Flora Woellner compares this to soaking in a tub of warm water, letting our body absorb the calming, cleansing effects of the water. As an example, take a moment just to soak in the truth of Psalm 36:7, 9: "How precious is your steadfast love, O God, all people may take refuge in the shadow of your wings . . . for with you is the fountain of life; in your light we see light." Charles Wesley prays in a song, "Unlock the truth, thyself the key, unseal the sacred book."

Commit some verses, or chapters, to memory if you can. One day you might be blind or disabled by a stroke or wired up following a car accident and you cannot hold a Bible! You also have nights you cannot sleep, or times you must sit and wait. The psalmist said, "On thy law I meditate day and night."

The Lord's Supper

Of all the strengths of frontier Methodism, its revivalistic legacy, and its circuit-system polity, the greatest loss was the spiritual grace associated with the sacrament of the Lord's Supper. Only the African-American children of Wesley kept the sanctity and theology of Wesley regarding Holy Communion. Most rural churches moved the Lord's Supper to quarterly usage and casual spirituality. Indeed, for generations, there was lower attendance when communion was served that when "the preacher was preaching." That is not Wesleyan. Wesley insisted: "1) That the Lord's Supper was ordained by God to be a means of conveying to men either preventing or sanctifying grace, according to their several necessities. 2) That the persons for whom it was ordained are those who know and feel they want the grace of God either to restrain them from sin or to show their sins forgiven." 3) That there is no previous preparation necessary but a desire to receive whatsoever he pleases to give. And 4) that no fitness is required at the time of communing but a sense of our state or need.

Whatever the frequency and whatever the mode, one Methodist fundamental regarding Communion is that we invite to Jesus' table, not to a "Methodist" table. Therefore we have always had "open communion" with no regard for church membership.

We will never know the full meaning of Baptism and the Lord's Supper on this side of heaven, but in recent years, considerable consensus has developed around two terms. We believe that in receiving the blessed sacraments they are accompanied by a "holy mystery" of the Holy Spirit's ministering to us, and the "real presence" of Christ. The Eucharist is indeed a means of grace we neglect to our spiritual peril. Wesley cited I Corinthians 10:16, then commented, "Is not the eating of that bread, and the drinking of that cup, the outward, visible means whereby God conveys into our souls all that spiritual grace, that righteousness, and peace and joy of the Holy Ghost which were purchased by the body once broken and the blood once shed for us? Let all, therefore, who truly desire the grace of God, eat of that bread and drink of that cup."[13]

Holy Conversation

The entire cultural history of the West has made us loners. Almost every facet of our life discourages trust and soul-sharing. Even in marriage, so many couples realize when the children are grown that the two adults who once married each other, no longer know each other! We not only need a friend in Jesus; we need Jesus friends. Another profound insight of William Young in *The Shack* is Mack's asking Papa, Jesus, and Sarayu (who are his depiction of the Trinity), "Who's in charge? Don't you have a chain of command?" Jesus answers, "Chain of command? That sounds ghastly." Sarayu (the Holy Spirit) comments, "We are in a circle of relationship, not a chain of command. Humans are so lost and damaged that to you it is almost incomprehensible that people could work together or live together without someone being in charge. This is why experiencing true relationship [with God] is so difficult."[14]

At another point, Papa tells Mack, "It is all about love and relationship. All love and relationship is possible for you only because it already exists within Me, within God myself. Love is not the limitation; love is like the bird's flying. I am love." (As if on cue, the little bird in the windowsill flew up, up, and away!)[15]

During his Georgia missionary pastorate, Wesley's diary is sprinkled with almost daily references to time spent in "necessary talk" or "holy conversation." He eventually included this in some of his lists of "means of grace." In recent times this term has been morphed into "holy conferencing."

"Holy Conferencing" or conversation has two dimensions. One is reflected in the old adage, "great minds talk about ideas, mediocre minds talk about events, and small minds talk about people." Our lives are so enriched when we hear speeches and sermons or develop relationships that push our minds to new horizons and our soul to greater depths. In today's cybernetic world, we risk overloading our minds in trivia and junk.

In his sermon, "The Means of Grace," Wesley lists the objections he has heard to his insistence that "stillness" and "quiet" often deny us access to "the arrows that sink into our soul" through a preacher, a book, or a mature Christian. He encourages us who are more mature to reach out to the "babes in Christ" and the seekers. "Thus we may lead him step by step through all the means which God has ordained; not according to our own will, but just as providence and the Spirit of God go before and open the way."[16]

My mother often told me, "You are known by the company you

keep." Though she meant my reputation — and the likelihood of being influenced by bad habits such as smoking and drinking and using profanity — at a much deeper level, her advice is still more correct. If we hang out with people who are reading, thinking, praying, doing justice, loving mercy, and walking humbly with God, we will likely adopt that lifestyle and discipline as our own.

There is a deeper dimension in "holy conversation." This is the need to have a trusted confidant. Carlyle Marney, founder of a clergy retreat center called "Interpreters' House," wrote a significant book called *Priests to Each Other*. I transposed that years ago into "priest at your elbow." The message convinced me that every Christian needs "a priest." This might well not be a clergy person and certainly does not mean our need for a confessional booth in a church! This means someone who is a bona fide soulmate with whom one can exchange the journey of souls, the peaks and valleys, the doubts and fears, the joys and God-moments. Some movements urge the term and formality of "spiritual director." We need not get so technical—just someone we trust and can really be honest with!

Marney insisted that this should not be your spouse but someone more physically detached. That raises a word of caution. Your "priest" must be a person with whom we do not cross sexually tempting boundaries. Marney urged pastors not to choose another pastor of the same denomination. We always run the risk of betrayal, and denominational colleagues are more apt to yield to that temptation!

The point is "the heart is a lonely hunter" and we need to find someone who is not an intermediary with God, but a confidant. If holy conversation is the essence of these relationships, it is not either of us becoming more like the other, but both becoming more like Jesus.

Leonard Sweet has recently written an important book called simply *11*. He takes eleven biblical characters, gives them a psychological/theologically descriptive title. He then advises that each of us needs the counterpart of a Nathan the prophet, who will tell us what we need to know about our sins; a Jonathan who will be a true friend; a Barnabas who will be the "encourager;" a "little one" like Rhoda; some "VIP's" like Lydia and Lazarus, and a sacred place like "Jerusalem." From these relationships come many holy conversations.

Sweet always sprinkles his books with pregnant quotes, one of which in this book is from psychologist and author Larry Crabb: "The Church is a community of people on a journey to God." I often hear from clergy the sad words, "I have many acquaintances and no real friends."[17] Sweet cites Mark's word about Jesus: "Jesus appointed Twelve . . . that they might be with him." If Jesus needed twelve, why do we Christians think we can go it alone? Sweet describes God's "dream team" as the "Triple F's"—**Faithful Friends Forever.**

I think Wesley was onto something that might be even more necessary in the 21st century than it was in the 18th—the class meeting. Until the 1850s, those small groups were the essential socio-spiritual vehicle for Methodists. The Sunday school system unintentionally replaced it. Today we need to re-invent some version of the class meeting. We need holy conversation!

Fasting

Wesley fasted. Every Wednesday and Friday, he ate nothing until the afternoon traditional English "tea time." He saw food as fuel to provide him energy for his work, not as an indulgence to be enjoyed for its own sake. He never encouraged fasting to the point of harming one's health, but did see it as a spiritual discipline; indeed, as a means of grace.

For the most part, Methodism has neither taught nor practiced fasting as a means of grace. With the increasingly serious problem of obesity in Europe and North America, we need to look anew the stewardship of the body. Fasting undoubtedly is needed to cleanse the body of toxins. Our diet has far too many food additives, sugar substitutes, and trans fats. Fast foods and low activity levels are creating a generation of children who will have major health issues. If we do not see fasting per se as a means of grace, we certainly need to see temperance at the table as a means of health—physical, emotional, and spiritual.

Participation in a Church

In Wesley's lifetime, he never acknowledged Methodism as a church; to him it was a movement of renewal within the Church of England. He never allowed Methodist societies to meet at "church hours." He insisted that a means of grace was the Sunday worship service of the parish church. By the 20th century, Sunday morning worship had become the major paradigm for "building up the saints" in all denominations.

The Confession of Faith of the former EUB church affirms that the "church is the community of all true believers under the Lordship of Christ...the redemptive fellowship in which the Word of God is preached by men divinity called, and the sacraments are duly administered.... Under the discipline of the Holy Spirit, the Church exists for the maintenance of worship, the edification of believer, and the redemption of the world." Given this definition, the church belongs in this list as a "means of grace." Indeed God has used the Church, with all its human weaknesses, to be the vehicle of all the other means of grace, including Holy Scriptures.

Worship within the church lifts us beyond the church to God. Gothic architecture did that in the Middle Ages, but now we must use other means. Music is a marvelous vehicle—both instrumental and vocal. So is preaching. Few exchanges in one's life surpasses an honest preacher sharing with a congregation what he or she has experienced with God.

While the church is God's mission to the world, we err to see it as an end in itself. The sad mistake of the 20th century was to develop a sophisticated "church-ianity" that was not synonymous with "Christ-ianity." We developed "churchmanship" (male and female) rather that discipleship. We assimilated new members by placing them on finance committees and program teams when they were babes in Christ looking for soul nourishment.

Wesley's Final Word on 'Means'

"Remember also to use all means as means; as ordained, not for their own sake, but in order to the renewal of your soul...."[18] We do humbly believe that John Wesley is a mentor of merit who can lead us to a life well-lived if we learn from what he called living by the "means of grace."

Questions for Reflection and Discussion

1. Do you agree that our conversion enthusiasm and confidence will "leak out" if we do not practice some spiritual discipline? Do you agree that God can use various expressions of "practical divinity" as means of grace?

2. Would you add others to Wesley's list? (*Actually his own list changed from time to time. Reading his sermon, "The Means of Grace" would be a good way to follow his own convictions.*)

3. Which means of grace is most meaningful for you in your own journey?

4. Which means of grace have you been most negligent of?

5. What decisions have you made as you read this chapter regarding your own spiritual disciplines as "means of grace"?

Epilogue

This little volume is intended to be indicative, not limitingly definitive, and certainly not exhaustive. The best format would be to leave blank pages for you to write your own additional chapter of what is "fundamental" for you!

Too little has been said here about social justice. That is a dimension of perfecting grace that needs its own treatment in another volume.

Some have suggested that a Methodist fundamental is Wesley's sermon and subsequent denominational emphasis on what he called "the catholic spirit" and defined as "if your heart is as mine, give me your hand." This is indeed a hallmark of Methodism. However, in this small volume we chose to limit the fundamentals to those related to what Wesley called the 'scriptural way of salvation.'

My fondest hope is to hear that Sunday school classes, small groups of diverse names and settings, individual laity, and clergy will find these pages helpful. As the current pastor of Kallam Grove Christian Church which has Wesleyan doctrines, I can see usage for this book far beyond the confines of Methodism. Every Christian needs to "work out your own salvation in fear and trembling for it is God who is working in you, enabling you both to will and to work for his good pleasure" (Philippians 2:12).

May the Holy Spirit use this small book as a helpful tool in leading you to "a faith that will not shrink" but will inform your choices and, through God's grace, sustain you "in the gaps" as the seasons of life unfold. Let this be a springboard to deeper and better sources. May God lead you to a spiritual fulfillment where none of your desires is in conflict with the Spirit of the living God.

Endnotes

Introduction

[1] Halford Luccock, et. al., *The Story of Methodism*, Abingdon, 1926, 58

[2] An e-mail Bishop Carder sent to the author on Jan. 5, 2010.

[3] Albert Outler, ed., *The Works of John Wesley*, Abingdon, 1986, Vol. III, "On Laying of Foundation of The New Chapel" 585

[4] Edwin Mouzon, *Fundamentals of Methodism*, Methodist Publishing House, South, 1924, 16

[5] Ibid. 36

[6] Gilbert Rowe, *The Meaning of Methodism*, Cokesbury, 1926, 151

[7] Edwin Lewis, *The Faith We Declare*, Cokesbury, 1939, 117

[8] Robert Cushman, *Experimental Divinity*, Kingswood, 1989, 100

[9] Ibid. 188

[10] Ted Campbell, *Methodist Doctrine*, Abingdon, 1999, 19

[11] Cushman, 21

[12] Ibid. 186

[13] Randy Maddox, *Responsible Grace*, Kingswood, 1998, 150

[14] Cushman, 189

[15] Outler, Vol. II, "Catholic Spirit" 93

[16] Outler, Vol. I, "The Way to the Kingdom" 220-221

[17] Ibid. 231

Chapter 1: Methodism begins with John Wesley

[1] The term "rise" was first used by Wesley, then by Bishop Holland McTyeire in his 1886 volume, but lay dormant in Methodist nomenclature until restored in 1995 by Richard Heitzenrater in *Wesley and the People called Methodist.* [2] Luccock, Hutchinson, and Goodloe, *The Story of Methodism,* Abingdon, 1926, 58

[3] Methodist historian Richard Heitzenrater corrects those who define Wesley's "social holiness" as 20th century "social justice." He notes that Wesley was a political conservative who believed "acts of kindness and mercy and grace." Wesley was not a Liberation Theologian!

[4] Weems, Lovett, *Pocket Guide to John Wesley's Message Today,* Abingdon, 1982, 86

[5] William E. Sangster, *Methodism Can Be Born Again,* Epworth, 1938 (book title)

Chapter 2: Fundamental No. 1 — Methodists are Arminians — What is That?

[1] Richard Heitzenrater, *Wesley and the People Called Methodists* Abingdon, 1995, 26

[2] Outler, Vol. III, 556

[3] Jerry Walls and Joseph Dongell, *Why I Am Not A Calvinist*, IVP, 2004, 220

[4] Maddox, *Rethinking Wesley's Theology*, Kingswood, 1998, 39

[5] Outler, Vol. III, 542

[6] Outler, Vol. III, "Free Grace" 547

[7] Ibid. 555

[8] William Paul Young, *The Shack*, Windblown Press, 2007, 185

[9] Rick Warren, *The Purpose Driven Life*, Zondervan, 2002, 22-26

Chapter 3: Fundamental No. 2 — "Way of Salvation" Begins With God's Character — Love

[1] Young, 102

[2] Outler, Albert, *Theology In the Wesleyan Spirit,* Discipleship Resources, 1975, 63

[3] Campbell, Ted, *Methodist Doctrine,* Abingdon, 46

[4] Rowe, 152

[5] Young, 191

[6] Internet

[7] Wesley, *Explanatory Notes Upon the New Testament,"* Epworth, 914

[8] *The United Methodist Hymnal*, United Methodist Publishing House, 1989, Hymn No. 387 Chas Wesley

[9] Outler, Vol. I, 578

[10] Ibid. Vol. I, 229 "Way to the Kingdom"

[11] *The United Methodist Hymnal*, Hymn No. 339.

[12] Scott Jones, *United Methodist Doctrine: The Extreme Center*, Abingdon, 2002, 107

[13] Warren, 30

[14] Young, 191

[15] Young, 192

Chapter 4: Fundamental No. 3 — Preparing Grace — God's Love is a Seeking Love

[1] Lovett Weems, *John Wesley's Message Today* (Abingdon, 1982, 22

[2] George Matheson, 1982 (Hymn: "O Love That Will Not Let Me Go")

[3] Weems, 23

[4] Steve Harper, *John Wesley's Message For Today* (Zondervan, 1983, 39

[5] Rupert Davies, *Methodism*, Epworth Press, 1985, 85

[6] Outler, Vol. IV, 293 Sermon: "The Image of God"

[7] *The Book of Discipline*, United Methodist Publishing House, 2008, 46

[8] Walls, Dongell, 69

[9] Warren, *The Purpose of Christmas*, Howard Books, 2008, 22-23

[10] William Abraham, *Wesley for Armchair Theologians*, Westminster, 2005, 51

Chapter 5: Fundamental No. 4 — Sin is Real — The Evidence is Clear!

[1] Lewis, 111

[2] Outler, Vol. II, 170 Sermon: "Original Sin"

[3] Ibid. 172 Sermon "Original Sin"

[4] Ibid. 173 Sermon "Original Sin"

[5] Lewis, Edwin, *A Christian Manifesto,* Abingdon, 1934, 130,132

[6] Smith, H. Shelton, *Faith and Nurture,* Scribners, 1941, 44,46

[7] Ibid. 99

[8] Lewis, 134

[9] Outler, *Evangelism and Theology in the Wesleyan Spirit*, Discipleship Resources, 1971, p. 29.

[10] Outler, Vol. II, 184 Sermon: "Original Sin"

[11] Ibid. 177

[12] Harper, 33-35

[13] Ibid. 32

[14] Outler, Vol. I, 143 Sermon: "Awake, Thou That Sleepest."

[15] Ibid. 226 Sermon: "The Way to the Kingdom"

[16] Ibid. 258 Sermon: "The Spirit of Bondage and Adoption"

[17] Young, 158

[18] Lewis, 197

[19] Jones, 153-154 and 221-240 (Chapter 8, "Social Justice As Sanctification")

[20] Kenneth Carder, *Living Our Own Beliefs*, Discipleship Resources, 2003, 48-49

[2] Campbell, Ted, *Methodist Doctrine—the essentials*, Abingdon, 1999, 62,63

Chapter 6: Fundamental No. 5 — Saving Grace — Co-operant and Resistible

[1] Williams, Colin, *John Wesley's Theology Today*, Abingdon, 1960, 75

[2] Outler, Vol. I, 187 Sermon: "Justification By Faith"

[3] Sangster, William, *Methodism Can Be Born Again*, Methodist Book Concern, 1938, 101

[4] Rowe, Gilbert, *The Meaning of Methodism*, Cokesbury Press, 1926, 30, 42

[5] Davies, Rupert, *Methodism, 1985, 52*

[6] Davies, Rupert, *Methodism*, Epworth, 1985, 51-52

[7] Outler, Vol. II, 197 Sermon: "The New Birth"

[8] Ibid. 429 Sermon: "Marks of the New Birth"

Note: The reality is that almost every infant in Wesley's England was baptized at birth. Wesley's sermons, "Marks of the New Birth" in 1746 and "The New Birth" in 1760 cannot be synchronized with his father's "Treatise on Holy Baptism," which John Wesley published in 1758. Wesley never included baptism in what he defined as "the scriptural way of salvation," but he did include the new birth. He also did not include baptism as a "means of grace." Therefore, we cannot consider baptism a "fundamental." Wesley's doctrine of baptism remains debatable. We leave that to the scholars!

[9] Ibid. 199-202 Sermon: The New Birth"

[10] Abraham, 67

[11] Ibid. 66

[12] Harper, 55

[13] Young, 126

[14] Harper, 55

[15] Outler, Vol. I, 405 Sermon: "The Circumcision of the Heart"

Chapter 7: Fundamental No. 6 — We Can "Know Our Sins Forgiven

[1] Outler, Vol. I, 285-286 Sermon: "The Witness of the Spirit II"

[2] Maddox, 168

[3] Outler, Vol. I, 287

[4] Rupert Davies, *Methodism*, Epworth, 1985, 50

[5] Davies, 51

[6] Outler, Vol. I, 298 Sermon: "Witness of the Spirit II"

[7] Abraham, 11

[8] Maddox, 84-87

Chapter 8: Fundamental No. 7 — Perfecting Grace — One Day at a Time, Dear Jesus

[1] Outler, Albert, *The Works of John Wesley,* Abingdon, 1984, Vol. I, Sermon 9, 260

[2] Colin Williams, *John Wesley's Theology Today,* Abingdon, 1960, 167

[3] Nolan B. Harmon, *Understanding the Methodist Church*, Abingdon, 1961, 70

[4] Williams, 175

[5] Harper, 93

[6] Cushman, 46

[7] Outlter, Albert, *The Works of John Wesley,* Abingdon, 1984, Vol. I, 394

[8] Ibid, 395

[9] Ibid. 396

[10] Outler, *Theology in the Wesleyan Spirit*, Discipleship Resources, 1975, 73

[11] Harmon, 70

[12] Ibid. 71

[13] Outler, *Evangelism and Theology in the Wesleyan Spirit*, Discipleship Resources, 2000, 125

[14] Hillary Hudson, *The Methodist Armor*, Publishing House of the Methodist Episcopal Church, South, 1900, 110-111

[15] Outler, Vol. III, 74 Sermon: "On Perfection"

[16] Johnson Oatman, Jr.

[17] Carder, 63

[18] Ibid, 63

[19] Vickers, Jason, *The Cambridge Companion to John Wesley,* Cambridge Press, 2010, 205

[20] Walter Muelder, "Ethics and the Interior Life," *New Christian Advocate*, June 1957, 18-22

[21] Albert, Schweitzer, *Out of My Life and Thought*, Johns Hopkins University Press, 1933, 59

Chapter 9: Fundamental No. 8 — Mr. Wesley's "Means of Grace"

[1] Albert Outler, ed. *John Wesley*, Oxford Press, 1964, 347

[2] Ibid. 357-358

[3] Outler, Vol. I, 376-377

[4] Abraham, 111

[5] Outler, Vol. II, 165 Sermon: "Scriptural Way of Salvation"

[6] Outler, Vol. I, 396 Sermon: "The Means of Grace"

[7] Thomas a Kempis', *The Imitation of Christ*, Revell, 1953, 47

[8] Albert Outler

[9] Albert Outler, ed. *John Wesley*, Oxford Press, 1964, 356-357

[10] Outler, Vol. I, 380 Sermon: "The Means of Grace"

[11] James Montgomery

[12] Charles Wesley, *United Methodist Hymnal*, United Methodist Publishing House, 1989, 595

[13] Outler, *John Wesley*

[14] Young, 122

[15] Ibid. 101

[16] Outler, Vol. I, 396 Sermon: "The Means of Grace"

[17] Leonard Sweet, *11: Indispensable Relationships You Can't Be Without*, David C. Cook, 2008

[18] Outler, Vol. I, 396 Sermon: "The Means of Grace"

NOTES

NOTES

NOTES